HOW TO
BREAK
THE
VICIOUS CIRCLES
IN YOUR
RELATIONSHIPS

OTHER HEALING COMPANIONS

Good Grief Rituals
How to Forgive When You Don't Know How
The Secrets of Whole-Hearted Thinking

HOW TO
BREAK
THE
VICIOUS CIRCLES
IN YOUR
RELATIONSHIPS

A GUIDE FOR COUPLES

DEE ANNA PARRISH, LMSW-ACP, LMFT

Photographs by Richard Gummere

Station Hill Press

Published by Station Hill Press Inc., Barrytown, New York, 12507.

Text and cover design by Susan Quasha, assisted by Anastasia McGhee.
Photographs by Richard Gummere. © 1993 Richard Gummere.
Cartoon on page x by Jennifer Berman. © 1993 Jennifer Berman.
Cartoons on pages 30 and 65 by Marian Henley reprinted with permission of Carmen Syndicate. © 1993 Marian Henley.
Cartoons on pages 5 and 89 by Andrew Lehman. © 1993 Andrew Lehman.

Distributed by the Talman Company, 131 Spring Street, Suite 201E-N, New York, New York 10012.

Library of Congress Cataloging-in-Publication Data

Parrish, Dee Anna
    How to break the vicious circles in your relationships : a guide for couples / Dee Anna Parrish.
        p. cm.
    ISBN 0-88268-144-3: $8.95
    1. Marital psychotherapy. 2. Communication in marriage. 3. Interpersonal conflict. I. Title.
    RC488.5.P365 1993
    616.89' 156—dc20   93-4794
                                                                 CIP

Manufactured in the United States of America.

Contents

Acknowledgments

I'd like to thank my editor, Evan T. Pritchard, for his continued support and confidence, his contributions — "Breaking Through Vicious Circles," "Three Stages to Healing," and "Care and Confrontation" — and his editorial advice for this, as well as my first book, *Abused.* Such a delightful man to work with. To my dear friends and colleagues: Barb Tunney and Kay Robinson, thanks for your loving support and input; Dr. Bonnie Gene Ritter and Bill Irvin, thanks for your contributions.

And to my adult children, Diana, Dave, and Mary Carol, thanks for being the precious kids you are.

A very special thanks to Anastasia McGhee, for pulling it all together, and Charles Stein, for ironing out the difficulties.

Thanks, Dear Hearts.

Author's Note

My first book, *Abused*, (also edited by Evan Pritchard) a recovery guide for adult survivors of childhood trauma, focuses on the dysfunctional family of origin. Using case histories, it exposes unhealthy patterns in childhood and examines how they affect us today.

When I first started talking to people about this new book, *Vicious Circles*, I was asked if it would be on the same subject as *Abused*. Initially I answered, "No, it's about a whole different population," separating in my mind the cause from the effect, as many of my clients have done over the years.

Where was my head? Of course it's the same population! It is about the dysfunction in our lives—the addictions, emptiness, confusion, and frustration—and why it continues. Vicious circles are often like a wound visible on the surface: rather than stick a bandaid on top of it, we need to pull out the thorn—or, in some cases, dagger blade—underneath; we need to study our personal histories in order to have a vote in the way we will behave in the future.

A vicious circle of some kind underlies every kind of abuse, every type of dysfunctional relationship you could name. There are cycles within cycles; we have all been affected by them at some point. The question is—how do you avoid becoming a "carrier" of someone else's viciousness germ?

How do you stop the cycle? Healing begins with understanding yourself. This book can help you in understanding vicious circles, but you have to apply it to your own life so that the needed changes can be made. As William

Blake appropriately stated, "In order to escape from a prison, the first thing you have to know is that you are in one!"

Whether we recreate the same crazy patterns as our parents or create opposite crazy patterns, our relationships are in some way affected by our response to our family background.

With that in mind, let's look at abuse and dysfunctional families from a bigger perspective; let's talk about vicious circles.

Circles

A circle is one of the most beautiful of geometric shapes—with its smooth, perfect roundness that makes us think of sunsets, full moons, and other lovely things like campfires, merry-go-rounds, and mandalas. A circle suggests wholeness and warmth and also cohesion, safety, and protection. History tells us that both the pioneers and the native people of North America drew strength in forming a circle; pioneers in wagon trains often formed circles to save their lives; Native American war councils were also held in circles. It is no accident that King Arthur's table was round, as are our summit tables today, representing equality and trust. The wedding ring symbolizes love without end and this is truly a joyous concept.

But circles also have another connotation: they keep going round and round, always returning to the same point, never really getting anywhere. Dysfunctional relationships between two people often develop in a pattern that resembles a circle in this negative sense. This is the kind of circle I address in this book: the "vicious" circle.

The Carousel of Love

In my counseling work over the years, I have become acutely aware of vicious circles in the lives of my clients: observing them and attempting to help people break them is the stock and trade of the counseling profession. How many times have I heard complaints like these made by one partner to another: "I get angry when you withdraw, and you withdraw when I get angry." "I'm not interested in sex when you're not affectionate, and you're not affectionate when I'm not interested in sex."

1

Everything in life is always
in motion and in mutable
relationship to the whole.
Aeoliah

In my office, I have a little carousel that, when wound up, goes round and round, reversing itself back and forth with the momentum. I use it to demonstrate my point to my patients, and they watch it almost mesmerized as it continues on and on without end until I reach down and stop it.

The dysfunctional patterns in relationships are equally mesmerizing and self-perpetuating. They seldom stop all by themselves. We have to do something. And whether working with couples, parents with their children, or employers with their employees, identifying the problematic vicious circles is the key to resolution. It's hard to make changes when you haven't figured out what the changes must be.

Identification of vicious circles is not the only key to resolution, however, because people must elect to break the pattern and then take the necessary steps to do so. The "I do this to you because you do that to me—because I do this to you because..." syndrome is not easy to stop, especially when it has been happening for many years.

Such battles can continue indefinitely. Each partner sees the circle beginning with the other. This must be defused by emphasizing that it does not matter if incident x follows incident y, or y follows x. It is xy that causes the trouble and must stop.

Two Kinds of Vicious Circles

Typically, there are two kinds of vicious circles at work in most relationships. First, there is the circle that arises following a particular incident between two people. I call this an "incidental vicious circle." The second can be observed to arise over and over again in the life of an individual, relationship after relationship, like a chronic illness. I call this a "chronic vicious circle." If you dig deep enough, you will find that these two kinds of circle are related, and that it is the chronic vicious circle that leads to the incidental vicious circle, not the other way around

The Basic Structure of Vicious Circles

In every vicious circle, there is an initiating "cause" and a reaction to it. In incidental circles, the cause is usually something one of the parties says or does. It could have almost any character—something seemingly inconsequential or something more dramatic or actually threatening. Either way, it provokes a retaliatory or defensive reaction on the part of the second member of the relationship. This response forces the first party off balance, perhaps inducing them to behave in turn in a defensive or retaliatory manner, thus getting the vicious circle started. In chronic vicious circles, some such pattern will usually be evident in several relationships and will have recurred over many years in the lives of both parties.

The discovery of vicious circles in relationships is nothing new. Awareness of them is reflected in myths and legends from all over the world. Traditional stories and myths world-wide have recognized the circular patterns people get into—stories about warriors fighting something that no longer is there, for instance, reflecting the projection of early childhood traumas into adult situations.

Vicious circles can come up in any relationship, but they are more likely with couples who are highly polarized. Polarization occurs when one person develops a negative attitude towards something the other feels positively about, and vice versa. Traditional marriages where the male and female roles are sharply defined and mutually exclusive are prone to becoming highly polarized. For example, the father handles all money and punishment issues, while the mother handles cleaning, nurturing, and communication. Where duties are this specialized, it is easy for each person to fail to appreciate the other's concerns. It is also easy, when roles are specialized, for people to fall into a dysfunctional rut, where each person becomes weak and atrophied in areas of skill given over to the other person. The husband forgets how to cook and clean and never gives a thought to the contribution these duties make to his own happiness, while the wife is unable to handle money responsibly and fails to appreciate the husband's bread-winning labors. At the same time, both husband and wife become "burnt out" in their own specialized areas, becoming bored housewives and executives. After a while, neither can survive either alone or together, and a power struggle ensues.

There are many other ways couples become polarized, such as when one person's desires for sex or success or adventure or freedom don't match with the other's. Opposites attract, and that's how the world goes round, but if the differences become too extreme and communication breaks down, this natural course of things becomes a vicious circle.

This book first takes us through a series of case studies that describe vicious circles around sexual issues, the attack/defend mode, codependency, and others. Second, tactics are presented that can help readers break the vicious circles in their own lives.

In what follows, let us first explore the simpler type of vicious circle: the incidental vicious circles that seem to arise over specific, one-time "incidents." Later we'll look at how these circles are affected by the "chronic" circular patterns ingrained in our individual personalities.

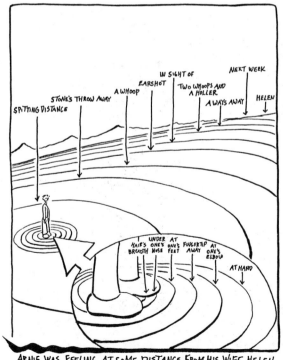

ARNIE WAS FEELING AT SOME DISTANCE FROM HIS WIFE, HELEN.
OFF THE DEEP END ©1992 Andrew Lehman

Incidental Vicious Circles

Most marriages can be improved 100% by working on uncovering simple (incidental) circles, locating their source, and making a plan of action to remedy them, to stop them in their tracks, or better yet, transform them into something more desirable.

Typically, these circles that make relationships so miserable stem from a single incident that becomes a habit. The habit develops into a pattern and then into a full-blown vicious circle and a way of life. It never seems so simple at the time, but a good therapist or self-appliable therapeutic technique like the one's described in this book can often cut through the confusion. How? Since there are only so many patterns you can fall into, and since couples have been falling in and out of love for centuries, the human race is beginning to catch on.

In the following chapters, I will recount some of the most common patterns of incidental vicious circles that I have encountered over the years. There are many more. You may want to add to the list yourself. I will also present case histories of couples and families along with the outcome of their therapy, some happy, and some not.

All names and other incidental information have been changed to protect confidentiality.

Attack and Defend

When couples get into this vicious circle of attack and defend, the result is chaos. He attacks and she defends herself, then she attacks and he defends, and visa versa. This goes on ad nauseam, and ad infinitum. It is so destructive that by the time they come for counseling , it's often much too late. I've heard many people say that "things have built up" until there are no feelings left.

I don't think fighting "builds" anything but resentment and instead erodes the relationship. All of the hateful words, ugly scenes, and actions, whether physical or otherwise, seem to take something away that can never be replaced. And it can start with (and remain balanced upon) a single incident. That's why the attack-defend circle has to stop at all costs.

CAROL AND KEN

Stop the Merry-Go-Round, I Want To Get Off

Carol and Ken: Background

This couple came in for the first session together, saying that they both recognized they were destroying their marriage. Both were bright, verbal, highly successful people in their respective careers. They had no money worries but they were in constant conflict with each other. Married six years, they had a four-year-old daughter and a fourteen-month-old son.

They had agreed that Carol would take some time off to be a full-time Mom after the birth of the youngest child. Their problems had escalated at that time.

There are many couples who come for marriage counseling as a last resort. It's as though they just stop by my office on their way down to the Court House. Carol and Ken were such a couple—from the minute they walked in, they were at each other's throats. Ken was so angry he kept getting up out of his chair, standing over me while he listed the *outrageous* things that Carol did to provoke him. All the while, Carol would sit shaking her head, saying, "that's not true," "wrong," "I do not!" He was being so threatening to her, I finally asked him to stop and notice how he was looming over Carol and me. I let him know that even *I* felt frightened. That seemed to shake him, and he countered, "I've never hit her....I've never hit a woman in my life."

"Well, Ken," I said, "you don't have to hit in order to be violent."

I took a chance on making him angry with me—he might have just walked out. But he didn't, he sat down. I told both of them that I wanted to talk a while. "You know, I've been sitting here just listening, trying to get a feel for the patterns in your relationship."

I reached down and wound up my little carousel, and they sat and watched it while I spoke. I didn't say a word about vicious circles or about the carousel. "As an objective observer, it's pretty clear what is happening."

I explained the attack-defend mode, and both agreed that it did describe how they acted out with one another, and simultaneously they pointed and said, "It's like that merry-go-round, isn't it?"

"Yes, it's like that merry-go-round," I answered, "and look how it perpetuates itself." They looked at each other and laughed. I talked about "disarming tactics" and "defusers" as a way to stop this crazy vicious circle.

Carol and Ken: The Issue

One of the issues they had already agreed upon as a major conflict point was that Ken typically came into the house and began making remarks about how little Carol had gotten done. She then typically became furious and began screaming at the top of her lungs that he had no idea about all the things she had done. And still at the top of her lungs, she would tell him what it *was* that she had done. And, if he ever did anything besides come home and "vegg out" in front of the TV....." and on and on, attack-defend attack-defend...

Carol and Ken: The Strategy

I asked Carol, hypothetically, "What do you think might happen if the next time Ken remarks on how little you've accomplished, you simply answer, 'It probably does look that way," nothing more?

She looked blank and speechless for a minute and then said, "I don't know." I looked at Ken and he, too, looked blank and speechless. I might have asked them what they thought would happen if they jumped into a den of lions.

Ken finally said, "Well, if she said that, I might say, 'You probably did a lot of things that don't show.'"

Carol said, "Yes, but I don't know if I could keep from getting mad."

"Why not try it," I said, "just for a week...just till you come back."

"And Ken, if Carol should jump you about anything, would you be willing to try to say something like, 'I'm sorry it seems that way.'?"

They agreed to try, but reluctantly.

I also talked about how threatening most "you" statements are and asked them to do the structured exercise using "I" statements in three categories: I regret, I request, I appreciate (see the section in 'Recovering' called 'Statements'). They agreed, again reluctantly, and left my office.

Carol and Ken: The Healing

They didn't wait a full week before returning, and when Ken and Carol came bouncing in next time, I thought it was a new pair of people. They were all smiles and told me they thought I was the smartest woman in the city of Dallas. That's what I love about working with highly structured folks. You give them homework, and they go out and do it...and come back to thank *you*.

What a racket!

Carol said that at first Ken seemed to be on his guard and made no snide remarks, so she didn't think she was going to get to try "defusing." But old patterns die hard, and the second evening, she got her chance. When she answered with her "rehearsed line," "It probably looks that way," humor came into play, and both collapsed in laughter. Ken said that the kids just stood with their mouths open. They'd been so used to the old battling, they didn't know what to think.

"I think that was the first time I really realized what the past year must have been like for them," he said.

11

*A loving relationship is one in which each sees the
beloved not as an extension of self, but as a unique,
forever becoming beautiful individual— a situation
in which the persons can bring their own special I
to each other, a blending of selves without the fear
of loss of self.*
                                                        Leo Buscaglia

As Ken and Carol exchanged their Regrets, Requests, and Appreciations, they really communicated. They cried and held each other—I got
pretty misty myself. This turned into a two hour session. They were on
cloud nine as they left, about to go out to dinner. It was the first time
they'd hired a sitter in nearly two years.

Much as I wanted to take the credit for solving their problems, I had
to tell them that they had done all the work. I also warned that it is quite
common for couples to fall back into the old ways, but they were way
ahead of me. Carol said they had already decided to continue sessions for
a while, "just to keep us straight," and so they'd have to report each week
that they had stayed on track. Smart cookies!

The Old Eggshell Routine

Couples get into The Old Eggshell Routine around many issues, when one or both partners walk around on eggshells trying to avoid a conflict or confrontation. Blended families, families where the parents are not both biological parents, nearly always find some of this acrobatic ritual going on. Needless to say, eggshell walking is not much fun.

Bob and Susan and Kevin and Kim ...

and the Eggshells

Background

When Bob and Susan first came in, I sensed the tension right away. Susan and Bob had gotten into another form of the attack-defend pattern that is very common in blended families. But this had become more than a vicious circle, it was more like a wagon train. As things unfolded, it became clear that Susan resented Bob's attention to his daughter, and he resented her resentment. He tended to "rebel" by doing things for the daughter, which fed Susan's resentment.

We're all very protective of our children and tend to defend even the slightest criticism, so the last thing a step-parent needs to do is to make their partner defend his or her child. In the first place, the defender can't see the situation as it really is, because he or she is too busy defending. Of course, the other side of this is that we tend to close off the lines of communication in this kind of vicious circle.

In the first session, Susan said, "When we were dating and then first married, Bob couldn't have been more wonderful if I had dreamed him up. Of course, that was before 'the little princess' came to live with us. When it was just Bob and I and my son Kevin, who was five when we met, we just never had a problem. Bob was like a real Daddy to Kevin, and he treated me like a queen. That may sound corny, but it's the only way I can describe our relationship. It was wonderful, and it lasted for two years. Then suddenly, Bob's twelve-year-old daughter, Kim, decided to come and live with us, and it all went to hell.

"Kim was a sweet enough child and, at first, she and I got along pretty well, but I guess I began to resent the attention Bob lavished on her—it was the attention I had become accustomed to. Then one day I realized I was getting left out altogether. He didn't treat her like a daughter; he treated her like a wife. That really upset me."

Bob and Susan: The Issue

Susan pinpointed the incident that triggered the cycle when she said, "I told him how I felt, and he told me I was being CHILDISH, which made me feel ridiculous, and also childish, of course, so I shut up about my feelings and the resentment began to build. It's been building now for five years. I've complained to Bob a few times over the years, but he's become so defensive that, yes, I do feel like I'm walking on eggshells. I hate it!"

Bob was in this first session, too, and listened without interrupting. I asked him to respond, and he began with, "I feel like a guy who's been screwing the maid, like I have to sneak around to spend time with or show

14

any affection towards my own daughter. It's absolutely crazy. I feel like I've been robbed of a natural, normal relationship with her, and I'm damned resentful. I don't think Susan is looking through the same pair of eyeglasses at her own relationship with Kevin. If I did half the things for Kim that she does for Kevin, I'd never hear the end of it. And, yes, I'm walking on eggshells too."

Bob and Susan: The Strategy

About the best one can do in the parenting of another person's child is to be supportive. Bob reported that he had long since learned that it was dangerous to voice any complaint he had about Kim to Susan. She typically threw back at him more complaints about Kim, which he promptly defended against. She also typically took the opportunity to expound upon how his parenting skills were surely to blame.

Susan countered that she thought she was being helpful and supportive and, after all, wasn't that what marital partners were *supposed* to do?

The fact is that we can be supportive of our partner without ever saying a word about the child. "I'm sorry you're going through this—I know it's tough. What do you think you should do? Is there something I can do?" are all supportive and appropriate statements, words that show caring but are not threatening.

Bob and Susan: The Resolution

Remember that expression, "To make omelets, you have to break a few eggs?" Taking each issue as it comes and confronting it gently, breaking the shell, as it were, may be the kindest way to live. Some conflicts do blow over by themselves, but not all. So asking someone if they are upset is a good habit, like wearing your seat belt all the time. You never know when a single incident can build into a vicious circle, or a whole vicious circus.

As I stated earlier, not all stories have a happy ending. In the case of Bob and Susan, too much damage had been done. The toxic interchanges had simply eroded away the feelings they had for each other, and Bob stated that, honestly, he did not feel able to work on the relationship another day.

They broke a few eggs, but too late for breakfast. The eggs were already too old. They separated and ultimately divorced. Two such nice people— it really hurt to see it happen.

Moms and Other Back Seat Drivers

At the risk of sounding like a sexist, I'm going to make the statement that women seem to be socialized from babyhood into the "Mother" role. Learning to care for babydolls and Teddy bears is, as a rule, our principal play activity. As adults, a considerable part of life is committed to directing children. Is it any wonder that we fall into the trap of "taking care" of and directing our husbands? At first they may love this kind of attention, but in the end, by the time they come in for marital therapy, most profess to hate it.

Margaret and Jay

The Green Light

Background

Married fourteen years, Margaret and Jay had four sons, whose ages ranged from thirteen to three. Jay was a successful dentist. Margaret had been a homemaker and full-time Mom nearly all of their married life. She had become pregnant three months after their wedding and had ruled the boys—by her own report, running the household with an iron fist—ever since.

Margaret and Jay: The Issue — Her Side of the Story

"He says he wants a divorce, and all because I told him the light was green," said Margaret during the first session. Jay came to the session with her but made it clear it was only because *she* had insisted. He sat very

Watch for little irritations, they grow into
destructive monsters. Verbalize them at once.
Anonymous

dutifully, looking at the floor, at my diplomas and certificates of licensure, or out the window.

"The light was green?" I asked.

"Yes," said Margaret. "We were sitting at the stop light, and when the light turned green, he didn't notice, so I told him. "'Jay, the light is green!' I said. You'd have thought I'd *hit* him!" she recalled. "He said, 'Goddamn it, I know the light is green, Marge.' He never swears—I don't *allow* it!" she continued.

After the "traffic light" incident, Jay was silent until they got home, and then he went straight into the bedroom and slammed the door, according to Margaret. Ten or fifteen minutes later, he calmly walked into the kitchen where she was starting dinner and said, "I want a divorce!"

Margaret and Jay: The Issue—His Side of the Story

"Jay," I said, "Why don't you talk about this? Let's hear what the marriage is like for you."

"I'd like to try, but what do you want to bet..." he said as he looked daggers at Margaret..."that she'll interrupt before I get one sentence out of my mouth and..."

"That's not fair, and you know it, Jay," she interrupted.

"What did I tell you?" he said.

I laughed and said, "Well, girl, looks like he's got your number."

She laughed nervously and said that she'd watch it. "Okay," I said, "Jay, you have the floor. And Marge, try to listen to his thoughts as though he were a stranger to you."

I asked Jay to use "I" statements.

"She's just so Goddamned bossy and negative..."

"Now I'm going to interrupt you, Jay," I said. "Start again, using 'I' statements."

He looked out the window. Marge started to say something, and I stopped her, asking her to give him time to gather his thoughts. In a minute, he started again. "I just feel like one of the kids when she talks to me in that tone of voice she uses, as though I don't have a brain in my head. God, how I dread coming home every day...I didn't even realize it until the other day. It's amazing how you can live with something for months or years and just accept it because it has become the norm."

This was a very articulate man once he started talking, and he made his points quite clearly. Margaret listened and seemed stunned at his words. This couple had stopped communicating a long time ago. His pattern was simply to withdraw into his own world or avoid contact in any way he could. Her pattern was to "call the shots," which made her feel in control, when in actuality, he simply tuned her out.

Since he didn't say anything, she just assumed that he was in agreement. This had worked reasonably well for them both until something snapped for Jay. A light came on for him (pardon the pun), saying, "I don't like the treatment I'm getting, and maybe I can stop it!"

Margaret and Jay: The Strategy

Endless arguments can develop out of small incidents. Of course, no one really files for divorce over a green light. We really must look at our

19

history to understand why in the world we have the notions we do about our own lives.

Why did Jay keep allowing Margaret to snip at him if he didn't enjoy it? Why didn't he confront her? If he did leave, what were his chances of falling into the same kind of relationship again with someone else? Why was Margaret bossing Jay—was it something that Jay did, or was it a habit? If she allowed him to leave, would she find someone "better" or find another Jay to complain about?

To answer these questions, I had to get them to talk about their individual histories. I asked Jay and Margaret to commit to at least one individual session before the conjoint sessions could continue. Both agreed.

To Be Continued....

I will pick up the story of "Moms and Other Back Seat Drivers," and what I found by digging into the past of each person involved, a little later in the section on codependency. Codependency is often the invisible cause of hostilities between two people in close relationship, especially when the issue seems to be microscopically small or even nonexistent. What's important is not so much the incidental vicious circle, but the chronic vicious circles of each individual involved.

The codependency question is more complex and requires more in-depth treatment, so first I'd like to address an area in which problems are often incidental and not too hard to resolve, and that is in the bedroom.

Ring Around the Bedroom—
Hide and Seek

By far, and indisputably, the most common of the vicious circles that I have encountered in my practice have been the ones around sexual issues. Perhaps this is because the feelings both men and women have about their sexuality are very sensitive and fragile. Although I do believe that men and women tend to view sex in different ways, each is equally protective where feelings are concerned.

There are vast differences in sexual need levels, and rarely do the needs match up perfectly. Even in the rare cases where they do match, there will always be a time when one half of the partnership says, "No thanks, not now." This can be, and often is, the beginning of a vicious circle in which the refusing partner feels pressured. Such pressure leads to obligatory yielding, and the internal dialogue goes something along these lines— "Well, I guess I'd better do it or he/she will get mad!" The reluctant partner begins to associate sex with anger, while the refused partner in turn begins to associate sex with deprivation. At this point, they are headed into a downhill spiral that often continues for years.

The fact is, that nothing obligatory is fun, even if it is something a person loves to do. When that something is an obligation, the joy vanishes.

JOHN AND KELLY

She Hides — He Seeks

Background

John and Kelly had been separated for a month before they came in for their first therapy session. She and eleven-year-old son, Matt, had moved in with her mom temporarily until she could get her thoughts together and knew what she wanted to do. John had appealed to her to come for at least one session and she had reluctantly agreed.

In their first session, I outlined my theory of vicious circles and asked them each to think about their patterns over the next week.

John and Kelly: The Issue — Her Side of the Story

In the second session, Kelly delivered the following tirade with a great deal of anger:

"I think our vicious circle started six weeks and ten minutes after the baby was born. Our sex life was always very good before we were married and in the early years of our marriage. We seemed to be compatible and have about the same sexual desires, and although I sometimes did it just because John wanted to, it was not a big deal.

"We were married for seven years before I got pregnant, and, towards the end, I gained a ton of weight and was absolutely, miserably uncomfortable. John seemed so needy at that time and used to badger me to have sex when he knew I didn't feel like it, and I would do it because he would

*You can love someone and still not do
what they want you to do.*

Catherine Ann Lake

pout if I didn't; and then it began to be a big deal. It was almost as if he became
obsessed with sexual needs all of a sudden. I think I really started to lose
respect for him at that time, but I kept thinking: after the baby's born, this
nightmare will be over.

"Well, the nightmare was not over at all. I had a very big baby and had
stitches all over the place and was sore as hell. When John came in my
hospital room, guess what was the first damn thing he said?

"'The doctor says we have to wait six weeks before we can make love,
honey.'

"'Make love!' God, that was the last thing in the world I wanted to think
about, and I couldn't imagine that in six short weeks I would be ready to
'Make Love!'

"During that six week period, I felt like John was watching the calendar
and marking off the days. He joked about it a lot and I laughed, but the dread
was mounting, and the thought of having sex felt more and more like a threat
every day. The soreness was going slowly away, but I felt like I had a
deadline.

"Besides the physical discomfort, I was *dog* tired. I was thirty-two years
old with a brand new baby—one who was up and down all night, like babies
will be. I was about twenty-five pounds overweight and I think that contrib-
uted to the fatigue, plus I had nobody to help me.

"When 'six weeks' rolled around, John announced that morning before he
left for work that this was going to be a 'special night.' Oh God! When he
was out the door, I sat down and bawled right along with my bawling
baby.

"That night *was* special. John brought home flowers and I appreciated that. I did try to get into the amorous mood he was in, but all evening, before I could get the baby down, there was a terrible strain between us. When we finally did get to bed, we didn't 'make love,' we 'had sex.' John was very eager, and I was eager to get it over with and very relieved when it was.

"That was eleven years ago, and it's been pretty much that way ever since. Only in the past few years had it gotten to be a real resentment for me. I can't understand it—I used to enjoy sex with John *so* much, and he's still attractive to me, and I do still love him, but when he approaches me now, I just bristle and generally say, 'AGAIN?' or 'God, is that *all* you ever think about?' Then he gets mad and slams the door or something equally stupid. But, when he comes back, I always give in, but I never enjoy it any more.

John's mouth dropped open as if he knew nothing about her feelings, which was a surprise to me. Was it possible that she had never let him know how she felt about this most important issue? It was possible, they both reported: she never had.

John's first reaction was disbelief, then anger. He had nothing to offer and got up and walked out of my office after about one half of the session. Kelly stayed and talked about her plans for divorce, and when she left, I assumed that I had seen the last of John and Kelly.

John and Kelly – His Side of the Story

A few days later, I got a call from John. He wanted another appointment. When they arrived together, I was somewhat surprised. I had no idea where all this was going. John stated that he wanted a chance to present his views. He had given the subject a lot of thought—and had given Kelly's feelings a lot of thought, too—and conceded that it was understandable that she felt as she did. Needless to say, his own view was quite different:

"I loved the time we had together before Matt was born, and I wasn't sure how I felt about having a baby, but Kelly wanted it very much, so I guess I sort of reluctantly went along with the idea...only Kelly didn't know how reluctant I was. All the time she was pregnant, I worried about how different our lives were going to be.

"Kelly already seemed to be losing interest in sex, and that had been very important to us—it was the way we felt close. I guess I did pout, and yes, I guess I did get angry. And Kelly, I'm sorry for that. I wish I could take that time back and change it. But, God, all I wanted was some affection and attention, and I guess I felt that the baby had taken my place. I began to resent him almost immediately.

"As Matt got older, it seemed like you just spoiled him rotten. Here is where I see our vicious circles, Kel. I know that I'm hard on Matt, but if I'm not, I'm afraid that you will indulge the little monster to death! (They both laughed at this.) Don't get me wrong, Dee Anna. I love our son, but I do hate the way Kelly shields him and makes excuses for him. The more she does that, the more rigid and hard-nosed I feel, and then I suppose the more rigid I get, the more she shields and makes excuses for him."

John and Kelly: *Communication*

Kelly agreed this was probably what was happening—they had entered a vicious circle concerning parenting as well as sexual pressure. John agreed that the sexual issue was exactly as Kelly had described it. Somehow, their concessions to each other eased the tension and they both decided to try to talk to each other.

John said, "You know, you never allow me to hug you without pulling away."

"But John, if I give you any encouragement, it always has to lead to sex. I'd love for us to be able to be affectionate and cuddle and all that. Maybe if we could just do that for a while without you expecting anything in return, I might just *get* turned on again."

"But Kel, I'd love that too." I encouraged them to try a practice hug right then and there, and they did. I asked how it felt, and they both said, "...wonderful."

The very mind-set of both partners, over the years, had changed from pleasure for both, to John getting his needs met and Kelly feeling used. In the end, no one had their needs met. Once the focus was off their mutual pleasure, the whole circular pattern was perpetuated by resentment. With many couples, this self-defeating mind-set is so entrenched that it's not possible to change it. But this was an exceptional pair, and John was particularly exceptional to be able to endure what many cannot.

In order to stop the sexual circle, the roles had to reverse. I explained this, and they both agreed that would make sense. They also agreed that it would be difficult. I said, "You're absolutely right. Only you can decide if your marriage is worth the effort."

John wanted to know how long it would take if he just backed off and let Kelly be the aggressor. I answered truthfully that I had no idea.

He said, "I love you, Kelly, and I guess I can wait just as long as it takes." Kelly laughingly answered that it may take eleven years. John slapped his forehead with the palm of his hand, and laughing, said "Oh shit!"

John and Kelly: Strategy

John and Kelly were exceptional in many ways. They were both very intelligent, and, more importantly, they still loved each other in spite of their conflicts. They were able to discern love from pleasure. But maybe the most important element was that they were both able to see the humor in the crazy patterns they had set in motion.

Since they were already living apart, we decided to use the separation as a tool to rebuild their relationship. Historically, there have been two options when a marriage went haywire: live together and endure the misery, or divorce and speed up the misery. Separation was the period of time one needed to get down to the court house. But in the past several years, many therapists have been using Structured Marital Separation, complete with a contract, to help couples reunite. At one time I was using this method so extensively that I developed a "fill in the blank" contract (See the Marital Separation Contract in the Appendix).

John and Kelly elected to give their time-limited separation six weeks. They agreed to one weekly conjoint therapy session, and one date each week. Due to the nature of their problem, they agreed that there would be no sexual contact with each other, and no dating or sexual contact with

Everything that lives lives not alone nor for itself.
William Blake

others. Matt would remain with Kelly, but John would spend individual time with him one evening a week and have him overnight once each weekend. Financial and other issues were worked out. They agreed to the structured homework assignment for the next session and we were back on the uphill track.

The homework for the next week was one I ask all couples to complete. Using "I" statements, they first listed their "regrets," all those things they have done that were harmful to the relationship. This encourages each to identify and own his or her part in the dysfunction. They then list their "requests," and with these they must be very specific: "I wish we were happier" won't do. The "appreciations" come next and generally allow us to finish on a positive note. Oddly enough, when using this exercise, both partners often request or regret the same things. (This worksheet is included in the 'Recovering' section.)

John and Kelly: Resolution

John and Kelly's third session went well. They had already identified the sexual problems and the struggle around Matt, so their requests mostly concerned parenting, affection, and household issues.

Both had many "appreciations," which included the crucial issues—like values, trust, and respect, always a good sign. After making arrangements for their first date, they ended the session with a hug. This time, I didn't have to orchestrate it.

Their first date was a disaster, but I had warned them that it might be. Feelings were too raw and they couldn't keep from fighting. They both had sense enough to go home early, and when they came for the forth session, they tried to pinpoint what had gone wrong. They agreed that they had both been very nervous and fearful, and the emotion that often covers these feelings is anger.

The second date went better, but there was still a certain amount of strain. In the next therapy session, however, their sense of humor came to the rescue, and we had a hilarious time laughing about the teenage-like awkwardness they had felt. I think that was the turning point.

In the meantime, John's time alone with Matt was doing wonders for their relationship. They were *having fun.* Kelly had been instructed to STAY OUT OF THE MIDDLE of Matt and John's affairs, a hard job for her.

But as I told you, they were an exceptional couple, and she was able to manage it. There was an instant improvement in John's parenting skills—he'd had them all along, but the vicious circles had kept him from using them. Matt responded. Kelly responded. John responded to their response: instead of a vicious circle, it was now a precious circle of mutual support.

It was a happy day when about two weeks later, Kelly and Matt moved home. They didn't last six weeks apart, but that was fine with me. This super threesome came in for a family session, and it was gratifying to see that Matt was all over John. He didn't seem to mind at all. Kelly sighed and said, "What a relief!"

Eight months later, when I called and asked for permission to use their case history in a book, Kelly and John were as excited as a couple of kids. Matt exclaimed, "ALL RIGHT!"

Maxine

Dist. by Carmen Syndication #13

Ring Around the Bedroom (Part Two)—
He Hides and She Seeks

There are many variations on "Ring Around The Bedroom." Sometimes she hides and he seeks, and other times he hides and she seeks. Within these two scenarios are countless variations, and they often boil down to one incident ... and a lack of frank communication.

Julie and Dave

The Honeymoon

Background

Julie entered my office—she was a tall, slender, very striking thirty-year-old woman. She poured out the following story almost frantically and was in apparent distress. But she said nothing about herself.

In truth, she was a very accomplished lady. She was a successful film producer, highly regarded in a top-notch advertising agency, but I practically had to drag this information out of her. It seemed to be incidental to her, nothing of importance.

Julie's Story—An Unsolved Mystery

Julie said, "I don't know what happened. Dave was interested in sex before we got married ... not tremendously, but probably more so than I was. He seemed to enjoy being with me. He was always there and I seemed to be very important to him. That's why I married him in the first place. But it seemed that immediately after the wedding, everything changed. Even on the honeymoon, he wasn't interested in sex. I just chalked it up to the stress of the wedding and of the honeymoon trip. It was a relief to me at the time, because I was so exhausted from the wedding myself. But after we were home and all settled in, it began to sort of worry me that Dave had changed so. It wasn't that I actually missed sex, but I was beginning to miss the closeness that came along with it. I guess it was, in a way, symbolic of the chill that had developed.

"I got caught up in thinking that I must have done something wrong. If he did make love to me, he seemed to be doing it out of obligation, and even then, it only happened a handful of times during the first six months or so.

"One evening, he came in, and I confronted him with my feelings, and he denied that anything was wrong, saying that I was making a big deal out of nothing.

"I kept at him about it until he got mad and stormed out of the apartment. I was frantic and cried myself to sleep. I woke up at about midnight, and he still wasn't home. Then I really got crazy.

"I called his parents and his brother and best friend, but no one had seen him. Just as I was hanging up the phone, Dave walked in the door. I was so glad to see him I didn't know what to do, but he was furious with me all over again for getting everyone up in the middle of the night and bothering them. He stayed mad for the next two or three days and would hardly speak to me, let alone touch me.

"I tried to tease him out of his anger, tried being seductive, tried making him feel guilty. I must have seemed just pitiful. We never did resolve anything, and the incident just blew over. Soon, we simply resumed that old superficiality, and I vowed never to bring it up again. I haven't.

"We've been married three years now though, and my self-esteem is all gone, and it's effecting my career and everything else in my life. I thought once about having an affair, but I think that would have been harder on me than the rejection. And, besides, with my self-esteem all shot, I didn't think anyone else would be interested even if I flaunted myself. I don't know what I hoped to accomplish by coming to you, Dee Anna, but I don't seem to have any friends any more. I didn't have anyone to talk to about all this, and I'm feeling so desperate.

Julie's Past

Once she talked about her history, it became clear that Julie had recreated in her relationship with Dave that which was familiar from her home life. Her parents divorced when she was eleven years old, and Julie was heartbroken. She described her daddy as a real charmer. He was a handsome, funny guy who played with her and teased her whenever he was around, which was rare. He promised her the moon and gave her nothing.

Before the divorce, and all through her early childhood, Julie idolized Daddy, waiting for him to come home and, more often than not, being disappointed when he didn't. She still remembers him calling to tell her mom he would be home "in a little while" and then not showing up until long after Julie was in bed asleep, if at all. She also remembers her mother crying a lot but didn't understand that it was because Daddy was out partying and because she suspected there were other women in his life. Of course, Mom was right.

Daddy left and went to live with his twenty-three year old secretary at one point but returned a few weeks later, full of promises and apologies. Julie was ecstatic. He would carry her around on his shoulders and tell her what a beautiful little girl she was. He would call her his little princess, and she felt wonderful.

A few months later, he was gone again. Julie couldn't believe it. She was sure that it must have been her fault that Daddy kept leaving. When he tried to return again, Mom said no, and ten-year-old Julie was furious and now blamed her for his leaving. The summer in which the divorce was finalized, she didn't see her father for seven months and didn't understand why. She still blamed her mother.

Daddy finally called before the holidays and promised Julie that he would come home and pick her up soon. He told her of all the things they were going to do together, and of all the gifts that he planned to buy her for Christmas. She believed every word and was so excited she told all her friends, and her mom, all that Daddy was going to do.

She began to "get the picture" when two or three weeks passed and there was no Daddy at the door. The next time Daddy called, it was after the holidays, and he apologized and made yet more promises. Julie was thrilled to hear from him ... but this time she didn't tell her friends, or her mom.

The relationship between Julie and her mother had been very strained for about two years now, and with Daddy virtually out of her life, she began to feel very alone and lonely.

Dave's Story — The Mystery Solved

"First I want to tell you that I'm pretty sure that most of our problems are my fault. I'm the one that's impotent. Goddamn I hate to say that, but it's true. I'm thirty-one years old and impotent."

He put his head down in his hands and stared at the floor.

"Dave," I said, "I'm not an expert in human sexuality, but what I do know about it from my graduate school days is that the biggest sexual organ in the body is right up here." I pointed to my head.

That seemed to break the ice for Dave, and he smiled a little and said, "You know, I've been thinking about that a lot lately. I've had enough Psychology courses to know, and I've read several articles in the past few months, and something has come back to me that I'd forgotten about. I guess it could have something to do with this mess I'm in. I hate to sound like an amateur therapist, but I know that I've had some resentment toward my mom because of the way she always treated me."

"How did she treat you, Dave?"

"Well, she was always so, I don't know, pure. I hate to even say this, but she was just so self-righteous ... Whenever I screwed up, she'd put me on this incredible guilt trip. I'm not saying anything against her, she did the best she could, and I didn't screw up all that much either. I mean, I was never a very rebellious kid. I generally was pretty compliant. I'd *learned* to be compliant through the years. Mom was never abusive in any way, but the way she controlled me was with tears. I didn't dare disappoint her or she'd get this horror-stricken look on her face."

He had to laugh when he thought about it. "Then she'd usually have

*I acknowledge that my real strength comes from
my ability to love and trust, not from my
abililty to perform.*

Philip Diaz & Patricia Gorman

to go to bed to recover. I guess that with some kids that wouldn't have upset them, but it sure worked on me. I grew up that way—guilty. There was only one way to do anything, her way. My poor Dad, he was so easy going—he just didn't make waves. And I never crossed her either, until it came to Julie. Mom didn't like her that much. The truth is, I guess she didn't like any girl I ever dated, but with Julie she couldn't compete.

"I really fell in love with her, and I still am. It's just that this damn sexual thing is driving me crazy!"

"How does your mom feel about your marriage now, Dave?" I asked.

"Well, that's the really crazy thing about it; she loves Julie now. She can't quit talking about how badly I treat her. She did an about-face the very day of the wedding.

"I remember at the reception, Mom asked to speak to me alone, and I was absolutely blown away when what she wanted to say was, 'Now that you are married, I want you to treat Julie with the kind of respect you have always given me.'

"She went on and on about my responsibilities as a husband and how marriage was sacred and all that. I can't explain it but I've never been able to feel the same about Julie since then. I mean, I love her, and maybe it's the old "Madonna Complex" I've heard about, where after marriage your wife just seems too pure to have sex with. Is that really possible?"

"Well, Dave," I said, "many things are possible when it comes to our minds. It's also possible that rebellion against Mom's attempt to control your marriage was an issue. But whatever it was, something made your feelings change, and a new mind-set was born."

36

Julie and Dave: Communication

I explained to Dave, "If a male feels he's unable to perform sexually, it's much like a chain reaction and it only takes one or two times. Then the fear that he *can't* perform can cause him to *not* perform. This causes more fear and doubt, and another vicious circle is born. Then when his partner begins to feel like a wounded bird, the pressure to perform feeds the whole crazy pattern."

I strongly suspected that Julie's "wounded bird" feelings had much more to do with hurt pride than the need for sex, and she confirmed that. In my experience, if most women were forced to choose between intercourse and cuddling, they would overwhelmingly choose the latter. Julie confirmed this as well in the next session, which she attended with Dave, their first conjoint meeting.

I asked him to repeat to Julie the conversation he had with me, and she listened carefully. She'd been asked to keep an open mind. When he was finished, she was quiet, but thoughtful for a few minutes.

Finally, she said, "It sounds like she sabotaged me. I just never thought about anything like that, but it makes perfect sense.

"Dave, I could do without sex forever, I guess, but I don't think I can do without the affection."

Dave said, "Well, I've always wanted affection too, but I guess I was scared you'd expect more and maybe scared I wouldn't be able to *do* more."

We talked about the concept of vicious circles, and Julie broke out laughing. "I kept it going myself by feeling rejected even if I didn't say a word." But it takes both partners to keep a vicious circle going, and both to stop it.

I used a little "Paradoxical" strategy when I gave them homework for the next week. They would be able to touch each other, but not sexually, and absolutely no intercourse. Both were to try to relax and pretend they had just started dating. They agreed to try.

Julie and Dave: The Healing

I wasn't sure what to expect, but I was not too surprised when, at the next session, they came in holding hands and smiling and told me that they didn't think they needed to make another appointment. Enough said.

Chronic Vicious Circles

Chronic vicious circles may be triggered by specific incidents, but they are actually based on long-unresolved conflicts within one or both individuals. Some of the examples we'll look into might be called: Moms and Backseat Drivers Revisited, Like Father Like Son, Love Abuse, and Codependent Ping-Pong. Each involves some form of codependency, but what's that?

What's All the Hoopla About Codependency?

Since codependency seems to be the self-help flavor of the month, no book about relationships would be complete without addressing it. But what is it? Many people are confused. (Many therapists are confused!)

I ran across a cartoon the other day by Buddy Hickerson that described the writing of the "Declaration of Codependency": We, the inseparable unhappy couple, do hereby vow, in order to keep a more pathetic union ... to continue hanging around each other ..."

I made copies for my therapist friends and we all have it hanging on our doors—in reality, most of us are codependents ourselves. Anne Wilson Schaef has stated that most mental health professionals are untreated codependents, and I guess it stands to reason. People don't generally get into the helping professions without wanting to "fix the world."

Codependency 101

The term codependency was first used in the Twelve-Step Program, and first appeared in Janet G. Woititz's book, "Codependency, An Emerging Issue." It was later popularized in Melodie Beattie's book "Codependent No More." The concept of codependency identified the fact that it is not only the person suffering from a destructive addiction that has a "problem." There are people close to the addicted person who are psychologically dependent upon the situation as well. These people are codependents. These are people who will do anything *rather than confront or abandon the addicted person with whom they are codependent.*

There seem to be two kinds of codependents; first of all there are those who are in denial about the other person, and who in some way make their continuing "high" possible, through making alibis, excuses, and fixing the results so they can do it again. These are the "enablers." Secondly, there are those who are "missionaries," who are so absorbed in solving the problems of the other person that they never take time to figure out their own lives. Both types become stuck to the addict like glue. The first type must cover for the addict because they can't or don't want to end the relationship, while the second type wouldn't know what to do with themselves if they weren't struggling to "save" someone else. In either case, the answer to the question "Is it worth it?" will always be "NO!"

A child of an alcoholic is often found to be a talented codependent; either an "enabler," reacting out of a need for love, stability, and security from the drinking parent and unable to stand up to the abuse that goes with drinking, or a "ball buster," continually making choices for the parent, controlling him or her, fixing things up, fixing everything but the cause, rather than letting the parent "hit bottom."

It has been found that those children often grow up to be "ACOAs," Adult Children of Alcoholics. This means they never left that role and usually married alcoholics in order to continue their enabling or missionary role, even if it meant misery and shame for everyone involved. A whole set of obsessive-compulsive behavior responses have been identified among people dealing with alcoholics, and this is what is now called "codependency." The dysfunctional family has been identified.

More recently, the concept of codependency has been extended beyond the circumstances surrounding chemical addiction. Anne Wilson Schaef and other psychologists have applied the addiction-codependency model to life processes, such as relationships and religion, and the parallels have seemed so convincing that the idea has caught on that anyone might be codependent. Today, many feel we live in an escapist, addictive, dysfunctional society, a society where the majority are either addicts or their compulsive victims. Meanwhile, the definition of codependence keeps expanding.

Are Homemade Cookies a Sign of Codependency?

I heard this description of codependency recently and I'm not sure who to attribute it to, but I think it has been said in various forms by many: "We are the rescuers, the enablers, the fixers of the entire world. We

> *Tryng to please is another form of trying to change. Love accepts.*
>
> **Hugh Prather**

anticipate the needs of others and set about to provide. We nurture, make better, solve, attend to, and fuss over, and we do it all so well. We are the caretakers." The trouble with this kind of caretaking, however, is that we give at our own expense (especially when we know it's not worth it) and are unable to allow others to reciprocate, leading to resentful feelings on both parts.

I've heard others say that we're carrying this "codependency thing" to the extreme. After all, what's wrong with being thoughtful and doing nice things for others? If we wipe out codependency, will we never again have homemade cookies?

Well, we don't want to give up the cookies, but there is a healthy balance between being thoughtful and caring and still allowing others the privilege of doing for themselves. It's one thing to "do something" and quite another to "do everything." It's yet another to derive all our pleasure and self-esteem in life from cleaning up someone else's mess.

My sense is that in the kind of crazy vicious circle codependent people enter into, each partner in the relationship is dependent upon the other to maintain a very dysfunctional pattern. Pia Mellody adamantly states that both partners in a codependent relationship are the product of immaturity and failed development as a result of childhood trauma. It is not surprising that they recreate other kinds of abusive relationships as they go on.

Moms and Other Back Seat Drivers—
Revisited

Our love relationships are usually patterned after our parents. There are exceptions, of course, but it's amazing that most of what we learn about how to behave, and what to think about ourselves and others, is learned when we're tiny little things, before we have reasoning skills and can be selective about the messages we receive. Therefore, if our mothers nagged our fathers and our fathers retreated into an invisible hole, does that mean we purposely avoid such miseries in our own relationships? Not often. It may sound strange, but we tend to repeat our parents' behavior, even if we hate it.

Margaret and Jay

Two Fronts Converge

Background

You remember Margaret and Jay, the couple that was getting a divorce over a green light? He said nothing about her nagging for years and suddenly wanted to leave. When they started talking about their individual pasts, many puzzle pieces fell into place, and a picture emerged of codependency and chronic responses.

Margaret and Jay: Jay's Story – Dad

"There's not much to tell you about my background. I had a good childhood, I mean. I was not an abused kid or anything like that." He was ready to stop right there, but I prodded him on about the emotional environment he remembered.

"Well, there really wasn't an emotional environment," he answered. "My dad was gone most of the time. He was a dentist too and worked long hours. He was also a golfer, so when he wasn't working, he was generally on the golf course, or at a professional meeting. There were *lots* of professional meetings."

I asked Jay if his dad taught him to play golf, and he just laughed, "My dad had no time for me. I used to beg him to take me with him, but he would either get mad at me for pestering him, or he'd say 'maybe next time', but he never did take me. I finally just quit asking. I guess you might say he was a rather self-absorbed man. But he was a good provider, as my mother always said."

Margaret and Jay: Jay's Story – Mom

"How did your mother treat you, Jay?" I asked.

"Oh Hell, I was her life. I had a brother who was nine when I was born, and he was a real problem. God, he was into drugs from the time I can remember. And he was always in trouble. My mother used to rant and rave at him and he'd just ignore her.

*There are times when you may want to give up on
a relationship, but never give up on relating.*

Leo Buscaglia

"My dad had no control either. I think that's why he stayed gone so much, or maybe because he stayed gone so much is why he had no control. I don't know.

"Now that I think about it, Mom really did raise us by herself. I remember her yelling to Dad about that fact, and I always just tried to get out of there. I hated hearing the yelling and nagging—Dad did too. He'd just leave. I don't remember him ever talking back to her any more than I did. We both hated conflicts."

This pattern just followed Jay into his marriage. When Marge took control, Jay was relieved and just allowed it, withdrawing into his own world as his dad had done, and as he had been doing all his life.

Margaret and Jay: Marge's Story—A Broken Home

"I didn't have much of a childhood, my dad was an alcoholic. What I remember is that I was just a small adult. I was the eldest of five kids, and as far back as I can remember, I was responsible for all of us. Mom worked because Daddy couldn't seem to hold a job. I guess sometimes she must have had two jobs or maybe three, I don't know, but she was never home. Daddy wasn't either, so I just took over. I don't remember anyone ever telling me I had to or what to do, I just seemed to know.

"When I was eight, my brother seven, twin sisters six, and little brother five, my mother came home one night, hysterical because she'd gone to the bar where Daddy hung out, and he got so mad he told her to go home, and that he was going to come and beat the shit out of her.

"She was scared to death that he'd hurt us kids, so she said. So I herded everyone into the car along with my mother...can you imagine this scene, an eight-year-old? I was pretty hysterical too, but I was able to grab a few clothes. I remember going back into the house to get a loaf of bread and a package of bologna. I was *so* scared.

"We got away that night and went to my grandparents' house, and I felt so relieved. They praised me for being able to take charge, and I remember the proud feeling I had, hearing that praise.

"But the next day, Daddy came and talked Mom into coming back home, and I don't know what I felt then. I wasn't angry, I don't think, maybe betrayed. That scene was repeated maybe a half dozen times over the next two years before Mom *finally* was able to refuse him and make a break for good.

"I was ten by that time and was largely responsible for the house and the little kids while Mom worked. I guess I've been responsible ever since."

Margaret and Jay: Communication

Given the history of Jay and Marge, it's not too surprising that their relationship had progressed to its current state. Both were able to see the similarities in their childhood patterns and the way they currently interacted.

Jay conceded that a divorce was really the *last* thing he wanted, but some drastic changes had to occur. I asked him to consider what kinds of things he'd be willing to take off Marge's shoulders, and her to think about what she'd be willing to give up. She said that she'd be thrilled to do that.

She also agreed to be more aware of her tone of voice and the manner in which she addressed Jay, and the children too, for that matter. He was to try to be more involved.

They returned the following week and each said that the other had made great efforts at change, and that they were doing much better. They continued coming for a few more times until each was reasonably satisfied.

Margaret and Jay: Resolution

Most of us can unlearn old ways and relearn new ones. At first it seems forced and foreign, but it's just like learning any new skill. If we want to learn to play the piano, or tennis, or anything else, how do we have to do that? Practice. And with time, it becomes automatic. New behaviors are the same as learning any other skills and can also be learned.

If Jay had just left and not sought some deeper answers in therapy, he would have been prone to either dragging out his problem forever, or falling into the same relationship he had with Margaret, with someone else, and so might she.

Like Father, Like Son
The Intergenerational Cycle of Abuse

Much of what we learn about how to interact and communicate also occurs when we are very young children, before we have reasoning skills, and before we can selectively make judgments about how to interact. Some people are able to recognize the dysfunctional patterns in which they were raised and make changes. However, many others simply repeat and perpetuate the intergenerational cycle of abuse.

KEN AND SUZIE:

Alienation

Background

Ken was a bright, verbal, very insightful but nervous twenty-six-year-old man who presented (came into therapy) due to his inability to be affectionate. He'd been married for three years to beautiful twenty-six-year-old Suzie.

Ken and Suzie: The Issue

"I just love her to death," Ken said, "but we've had this running battle since before we were married. I just can't do what she needs me to do, and she thinks I'm a cold, stubborn bastard. She says I withhold affection from her just to be mean, when I know how important it is to her. But I

> *Unconditional love means learning to separate*
> *the person from the problem. Love the person;*
> *work with the problem.*
>
> **Ken Keyes**

really don't, and I'm so afraid she's going to leave me. I don't think I'd want to live without her."

"Well, Ken," I said, "I wonder what makes it so hard for you to be affectionate with a beautiful, desirable woman that you love to death," as if I couldn't guess.

"Oh, I know exactly what," he hurriedly told me. "I came from a very cold, unaffectionate family. I never saw my parents hug or even touch each other, and they certainly didn't hug or touch me or my brothers. Especially my Dad. He thought it was unmasculine to treat boys like little "sissies.""

"What do you think, Ken?" I asked. "Do you think it's unmasculine for a man to be affectionate with his wife and kids?"

"No," he said, "I don't think that in my head at all. As a matter of fact, I think it's a weakness in me, but I don't know how to make myself do it—I don't know *how* to do it."

"Well," I said. "In that case, I think it'll be a piece of cake." He relaxed a little, I was glad to see.

Ken and Suzie: Communication as Strategy

"What kinds of things would Suzie like to see happen specifically?" I asked.

"She'd like to be hugged without having to ask me, and I have tried to do that, but it felt so weird and I was so embarrassed. Then she got mad and said that if it was such an effort for me, that she didn't even want me to bother. Now I'm afraid to try, because I know I can't do it right."

49

"I guess I'm going to have to talk to that Suzie girl," I remarked, "because she's going to have to give you a little help with this. Ken, just about all behavior is learned, and if we can *learn* it, we can *unlearn* it and relearn it in a different way. What you're talking about is simply learning new skills— social skills— which are no different than learning other kinds of skills.

"Remember when you learned to drive a car? How hard it was, and how you had to pay attention to every little move you made? Now you drive across town and don't remember how you got there, right? With practice, it has become automatic for you."

"Yeah, that's right...I guess," he agreed, "but it's different with Suzie. She's not going to like it if I have to *practice* on her."

"That's why I told you I'm going to have to talk to her. She will need to learn to be patient and understanding, without taking your 'arrested development' personally," I teased.

Suzie was more than happy to come in the very next day. After a brief explanation of what Ken and I had talked about, she said that she had never considered that Ken must learn to do something he'd been deprived of all his life. She agreed to be patient and let him know that she loved his attempts at being affectionate. If it seemed stiff and foreign to them both, well, so what? In time it would not.

Ken and Suzie: The Healing

They came in together two weeks later and I noticed how attentive Ken was to Suzie, but he did seem stiff, as if he were on stage playing a role.

Change is a volitional process. No one can change others without their consent. Any relationship that does not respect the individuality and choice of the other cannot survive.

Leo Buscaglia

If Suzie noticed, she didn't let on, although she confided later that she had noticed and was playing her own role. She did it well.

The next time I saw them a few weeks later they were smiling and laughing, something I had not seen with either of them before. Ken told me that he couldn't believe how easy it had become to show affection, and Suzie laughingly answered, "Yes, he's become perfectly sickening. He's chasing me all over the house." Ken made an obscene gesture, and they left holding hands.

That was two years ago. I didn't see them again, but when I called to ask for permission to share their case, I found out they had a new baby. Ken got on the phone and said he'd really been intending to call me since the baby was born. He wanted to let me know that he did not intend to repeat with his own little son the childhood treatment he'd been subjected to. Now that's a success story!

*Even though you are only half of a
relationship, you must remain a whole
person, apart from the relationship.*

Anonymous

Love — an Abused Substance

In the codependent couple, one is typically the victim of serious neglect
and/or abandonment. In my experience, I've found that this is generally
the woman. She needs closeness, affection, attention, and approval and
has a dreadful fear of abandonment. She places so much time, attention,
energy, and value on her partner that she often becomes very isolated. Her
love for him becomes the content of living. If children are involved, she
may neglect or disregard them. Her partner literally becomes her "Higher
Power." She is known as the "Love Addict."

The other partner has a serious fear of intimacy, often as a result of a
too-controlling parent. Frequently, moms have a tendency to control and
protect their little boys, perhaps from an overly rigid father, or compen-
sating for an absent father. These little boys grow into men who have a
fear of engulfment, entrapment, enmeshment. They are withdrawn, silent
about their feelings, and terrified of their possessive partners. They are
known as "Avoidance Addicts."

These two, the Love Addict and the Avoidance Addict, find each other
like a couple of magnets. It doesn't take much thought to see the potential
for vicious circles here: the little boy in him continually seeks the protective mother whom the rebellious man will always abandon. One of my
clients who is an avoidance addict explained it very simply: "Who else but
a love addict would have chased me that hard?"

Greta and Jason:

Love and War

Background

When this twenty-six-year-old beauty walked into my office I thought she must surely be a model. She was tall and slender with gorgeous skin and eyes and strawberry blonde hair. I'm not usually so preoccupied with outer beauty, but this young woman was definitely a knockout. To top it off, she was as sweet and unaffected as anyone you would ever want to know. However, when she told me she was seriously depressed due to the breakup of a two-year relationship, I was not too surprised, since I see so many young women in her age group who describe a similar problem.

Greta and Jason: Greta's Story

"I met Jason in college and at first he was so pushy that I told him to "chill out." But he would not leave me alone. God, he nearly drove me crazy. His persistence became almost funny, and I have to admit it was an ego trip, so I finally agreed to go out with him. He seemed so adoring and was so attentive and just couldn't do enough to please me. The college guys I was used to dating had never treated me like that. He was also gorgeous. I began to see a certain air of arrogance that was a real turn-on for some reason. He became possessive and that was also a turn-on. He treated me like I was a precious person and that was, *of course*, a turn on.

> *You do not find yourself with this person by accident. You knew what you were doing when you formed the relationship, and you were not mistaken.*
> **Hugh Prather**

Role Reversal

"It wasn't long before I became enamored with him, wanting to be with him constantly. He was all I could think about and talk about. I realize now that my friends started avoiding me early on, but I didn't notice then. I probably wouldn't have cared anyway. Jason was my only concern.

"I don't know when things began to turn around, but that's just what happened. Somehow, in a period of six or seven weeks, I became the pursuer and he was the one pulling away. He had never wanted to talk about anything important like his thoughts and feelings, hopes and dreams. I had tried to pull these things out of him but he was not interested, and I usually had to talk to him over the TV set. He began to make excuses about why we couldn't be together and I caught him in one lie after another. He also began to flirt with other girls when we were together, and that just about drove me crazy.

"When I spoke to him about these things, he accused me of being 'a possessive, controlling bitch,' and he'd get so angry that I was afraid to open my mouth. I learned to tolerate his general attitude of annoyance and disapproval and his cutting remarks. I tried so hard to give him space, and I remember thinking, 'If I can just shut up, he'll stop withdrawing.'

"So I vowed not to question him any more. I was able to do that pretty well for a while, but I guess my facial expressions and body language gave me away, because he still thought I was trying to control him. I guess I was. I was trying to control him by being "better" in every way—better looking, better cooking, better in bed. I was buying him gifts and helping him with his homework, too. My own grades went to hell. He gave me just enough positive attention to keep me tolerating his rejections, but the more attention I paid him, the more I tried to control him, the more he pulled away. The more he pulled away, the more I tried to control, and the needier I became.

At this point, most of my friends were avoiding me like the plague because all I could talk about was my pain. I became more and more isolated, no Jason, no friends, even my mom began to be unavailable. When I could get someone to listen to me, they'd say, "Greta, get rid of that creep!"

"Next, I started trying to control him by withholding sex, with tears, with threats. I started spying and following him, sure that he was cheating on me, and, of course, he was. Eventually, I caught him and I was so crushed I thought I would surely die...and I wanted to. I had such overwhelming emotions.

"The pain was literally physical. I hurt so bad and cried so hard, not eating or sleeping. I was furious with Jason, and at the same time, fearful of life without him. I feared what my friends and family would think and how I was going to face them. And guilt—I couldn't stop thinking that it was my fault I'd lost him—if I just hadn't been so stupid.

"And here's the *really* crazy part. I'd been so angry and hurt that I cut off the relationship immediately. But guess what happened? Jason called and called and begged and begged me to take him back, swearing "things would be different." And for three or four days, with the help and encouragement of my friends, for they were now my friends again, I stood firm. But that damn manipulator wore me down and I agreed to see him, "just to talk." Of course, once I saw him, we fell into each others' arms, and I was hooked right back in again. Once again, I believed every promise he made and everything he said."

The vicious circle began again. Greta told me that this cycle was repeated eight or even ten times over the next two years. She was still struggling with herself because, once again, Jason was calling and calling and begging and begging, telling her he didn't want to live without her. He wanted her to move in with him and swore that if only they lived together, everything would be different.

"RIGHT!" I told Greta. "It will be different, but not the way you have in mind."

Greta and Jason: Greta's Past

We talked at length about codependence, love addiction, and the vicious circle she and Jason had been in for more than two years. She was astonished that her painful affliction had a name. She thought she was the only one in the world who was so obsessed with another person.

We also talked about her early childhood treatment. As I mentioned earlier, I believe this is the primary cause of adult emotional disturbances.

Greta told me that her parents divorced when she was a baby, and she'd only seen her dad two or three times in her life. He'd moved off, she didn't remember where.

I told her I was not surprised that she had some abandonment issues, and she quickly took offense to that. "Well, it wasn't that he didn't want to see me, he was in a business that required a lot of travel, and there was no work in his field where Mom and I lived. Besides, I had an okay childhood. Mom was great.

"The only thing was that she had to work so hard because Dad couldn't afford to help us financially. He had remarried and had his own family to support, so I didn't get to be with Mom very much.

"I remember crying a lot when she had to leave me at the babysitter's. I hated that old woman. But that was just when I was little. When I got older, about nine or ten, Mom let me stay home alone after school, and that was better. Except when she had to work nights—that was pretty awful, because I was scared.

"And then, of course, sometimes she had to work weekends, but she really didn't have any choice about that. When we were together, she was wonderful."

Greta agreed to do some reading and return the next week, and about Jason, she agreed to do *nothing*.

She didn't do exactly nothing about Jason. When he called her, she told him that she'd seen a therapist and was not supposed to make any decisions at all.

Jason said, "Great, I'll go with you!"

Greta, who was so used to allowing herself to be manipulated by this steamroller, said, "Okay."

She called to tell me the plan, but I said, "NOT okay, Greta. This is your therapy, and it has nothing to do with Jason at this time. But I will agree to see him individually to find out what his issues are, and then maybe down the road we can all get together."

She agreed, and Jason would have agreed to anything at that point, because avoidance addicts have an underlying fear of abandonment themselves, which is what keeps the vicious circle going.

Greta and Jason: Jason's Story

"I'm afraid I've really screwed it up this time. I love Greta to death. She's the sweetest thing in the world. I don't know what in the hell gets into me to make me treat her like I do. Except that she's like a bottomless pit. Sometimes, I feel like I'm being swallowed up and it makes me crazy. I just want to get away from her, except that when she wants to leave *me*, I panic. I feel like I'm going to die. I can't think or work, and I make an awful ass out of myself. All her friends hate me, and all mine think I'm crazy."

Jason put his head down in his hands and said, "I think I'm crazy too."

Greta's not the only victim in this couple. The needier she is, the more Jason pulls away, and the more he pulls away the needier she becomes. On the grander scale, she chases him and he runs away until she gets enough and runs from him. At this point, he must then chase her until he can persuade her to start the circle all over again.

"Jason," I said, "I don't think you are crazy, but this crazy, vicious circle you and Greta are in must make you feel that way. Why don't you give me some background about you?"

Greta and Jason: Jason's Past

"Well," he said, "I don't see what my background has to do with what's going on now."

"I know you don't," I laughed, "but why don't you humor me?"

Jason laughed too. "There's not much to tell. My dad is an alcoholic, but I don't think that really affected me much. He wasn't a falling down drunk, or anything like that, he just drank a lot. And he never hit me or mistreated me in that way.

"Actually, I didn't really know that he had a drinking problem until my mom divorced him three years ago—I was nineteen years old. She told me then about all the abuse she had taken from Dad to shield my little sister and me. I guess I knew about it all along, but just sort of blocked it out.

I knew that she was controlling and would hardly let me out of her sight, but I realize now that she was trying to protect me. But as a kid she nearly drove me crazy!" he laughingly said.

"She's still pretty pushy!"

"Sort of like Greta, Jason?" I asked. He looked stunned ..."Well, uh ... yes ... I guess so. I never thought of that," he answered.

Greta and Jason: Intergenerational Circles

We seem to recreate the same emotional environment in our adult lives that we grew up with, even though we don't do it intentionally. It's the familiar, it's what we know—and we fear the unknown. Jason's mother had been over-protective and controlling, smothering him in an effort to protect, and he eventually found a woman who would give him that feeling of over-attention, one who'd chase him and strive for the emotional intimacy that he withheld, so that he could resist her as he had resisted his mother. Once he got her hooked in, Greta filled the role his mother had once played.

Greta recreated the abandoned feeling she grew up with. Dad abandoned her, and regardless of the reason, a child feels unloved because of abandonment. To a child, it doesn't matter whether Mom is working three jobs to make ends meet, as Greta's mother was, or whether she was out on the town, sitting in some divey bar. To the small child, mom is either there or not.

As an adult, she can rationalize, but the long-term effects of Mom's absence are already well entrenched. Greta was very protective of her mother, as most of us are. She was even protective of her dad, the deserter, with a rationalization that didn't hold water.

Greta and Jason: Strategy 1 – Loving Your Own Life

When Greta returned for her next session, she had done her homework. She had poured her obsessive-compulsive self into the books on Love Addiction I'd recommended. She had listened to Pia Mellody's tapes on Love Addiction and Codependency, and she had come back stating, "I'm a Love Addict, pure and simple! Those books and tapes described me and my life and it just makes me *sick*!"

"Well, you don't need to be sick, Greta," I told her, "because getting past the denial is the largest single step toward recovery."

"The only thing I can't understand is how I got this way—I don't think I was a *mistreated* child."

"We were all mistreated children, Greta," I said, "to one degree or another." None of our parents was perfect, and none of us is a perfect parent to our own kids. We all suffered traumas of some kind, traumas that caused long-term effects, and one of the most common reactions is obsessive-compulsive behavior.

Develop a relationship with yourself before
getting deeply involved with anyone else.
Ken Keyes

"Obsessive-compulsive simply means that we seem unable to control ourselves in regard to our addictive patterns. Some of the more common addictive agents include alcohol, other drugs, cigarettes, food, work, spending, relationships, and on and on. You and your mother got deserted, and the long-term effect on you is a fear of abandonment."

"But my mom didn't desert me."

"Didn't she, Greta?"

"Well, she couldn't help it. She had to work," she said.

"I know it and you know it now, but as a two- or three- or even six-year-old, all you remember is being left with that babysitter you hated. And then at ten, being left alone and frightened at night."

She was quiet for a long time, then said, "That old woman was so hateful to me. I can't tell you how much I dreaded every day for, I guess, eight or nine years. She was pleasant enough until after my mother left, so mom never knew how bad it was. I don't know why I never told her. Okay, so I'm past the denial—if that's the big step, what are the little ones?

Greta and Jason: Strategy 2—Communication

The treatment of any addiction begins with de-tox, and in the case of love addiction, detoxification consists of facing the abusive upbringing; talking about it, writing about it, and debriefing. I have my clients not only talk out their feelings about incidents from the past, but write letters to the people who have been destructive to them. Greta wrote to the babysitter first. She made a long list of the various incidents of mistreatment, and it was considerable. She also described how she felt as a child, and how the

61

long-term effects were influencing her life as an adult. In addition, she told the babysitter what she wanted from her now, which was an apology.

Of course, the elderly lady had been dead for years, so there was never a question of mailing the letter, but that's not the point. The therapy is in the act of writing it down where you can see it. Once you write it down it's hard to ignore, hard to deny, and easier to let go.

One half of the therapy is in the writing, and the other half is in the sharing. This is the "debriefing" stage mentioned earlier. Greta read her letter in the next therapy session and commented that she felt as if a mountain range had been lifted off her shoulders. I can't explain the therapeutic magic of writing—I just know that it works.

In her next session, she brought the letter she'd written to her dad. She was amazed at how angry the letter was. I wasn't.

Greta and Jason: Strategy 3—Letting Go

Bringing to light all the old resentment and then carrying it around forevermore is not the idea here. Bring it up, express feelings about it, resolve it, and then release it. Like a pressure cooker, if we don't let off some steam, we explode. The secret is to let the steam out a little at a time. It's not easy—it may be the hardest thing we ever do, but if we don't, we let the past ruin the rest of our lives. And if we deny the events in our conscious minds, we empower them to dominate our unconscious.

Greta and Jason: Strategy 4 — Self-Esteem

Besides working on family-of-origin issues, the Love Addict must begin a program to fill herself or himself with self-love, self-esteem, and self-care. Most people, when hearing this comment say, "That sounds awfully selfish."

That's the next order of business, changing the word selfish to self-survival. I give all of my clients the following list to hang on the bathroom mirror or fridge. It contains four steps to emotional growth:

1. Identify and eliminate those false beliefs about yourself that inhibit your self-esteem.
2. Make building your self-esteem a priority, surrounding your self with as many loving, encouraging people as possible.
3. Recognize that you are a capable adult with choices, options, and an ability to make changes.
4. Confront those people who have injured you. If they are unwilling to work with you toward a healthy relationship, decrease contact with them.

MATURITY IS A LIFELONG PROCESS!

Greta and Jason: Strategy 5 — Stop Controlling

If the Love Addict chooses to stay in the relationship with the Avoidance Addict, I tell her that she's probably going to have to be a very good actress, maybe for the rest of her life.

One of the things she'll have to do is to stop the toxic exchange with him:

1. She'll have to stop trying to connect with or control him through intensity—in other words, lighten up.
2. Stop trying to connect with or control through emotional interaction, tears, etc.—save the emotions for the therapist's office.
3. Stop trying to connect with or control through picking fights.
4. Stop trying to connect with or control through anger or threats.
5. Stop trying to connect with or control him by questioning. In other words, get out of his business—stop the complaining, the checking up on him, and all the rest.
6. Stop trying to connect with or control him through helplessness. Being pitiful is a turn-off.

With all the energy you'll conserve, get busy with your own life, and give up trying to make him change. Again, quoting Pia Mellody, "Exercise a 'wall of pleasant' and a 'wall of good manners,' having warm personal regard for all, including him, at all times. Tall order? You'd better believe it! But you may find you stop thinking about "winning him back," and start to win back your own life instead.

Greta and Jason: Resolution

Greta decided to have a try at interacting with Jason in this manner, and he did respond—at first. He returned to the way he had been in the very beginning, and at first Greta was delighted. She remained very careful to continue the treatment but got tired of playing a role. Deprived of the fuel for *his* role-playing, Jason became very angry with her, and they eventually parted company.

She involved herself with a new love, but not before she was independent for several months. She needed that time to heal and discover that she was a whole person without someone to be her other half. She tells me that Jason still calls her occasionally to talk about his problems, but now she has trouble believing she was ever actually involved with him in that painful, vicious circle that was their lives.

Maxine

Codependent Ping-Pong

As we saw with Greta and Jason, role reversal is a common thing among codependent couples, especially when love addiction is the issue. Remember that carousel that wound around first one way then the other? Relationship addicts are like that, the give and take of relating is blown all out of proportion.

Some couples have multiple issues and forms of codependency when they first meet and then begin role reversals, sometimes on several issues at once. It gets pretty complicated. The results can be comical or tragic, depending on the circumstances.

Dan and Jackie

Multiple Issues

Background

Dan initially came in alone to talk about his feelings of jealousy and insecurity in his relationship with Jackie. He'd been married to a very poorly functioning woman and had an eight-year-old child when Jackie came into his life. They almost instantly fell in love. He was very torn because, although he'd had no feelings for his wife for several years, infidelity was against his value system, and he idolized his little daughter. The whole situation nearly drove him crazy for about six months, he said. In the end his heart overruled, and he asked his wife for a divorce. He moved out and eventually moved in with Jackie.

Dan and Jackie: **Issue 1 — Control**

Until that time, they'd had no problems and their relationship had seemed "Heaven sent." They had been virtually isolated from other people because of Dan's marital circumstances, and both were relieved when they could bring their relationship "out of the closet." But Dan's insecurity began to surface when he saw Jackie joking and flirting with other men at parties and social gatherings, a side of her he had not known before. When he told her how he felt, she got angry and accused him of being possessive and controlling. She was a "highly successful, independent woman and would not be treated like some child," she said.

Dan's first appointment with me was soon after the confrontation described above. I didn't hear from him again for about a month. When he returned, he was literally pacing the floor in my office saying that he didn't know what to do. He was so in love with her, it made him miserable. When Jackie was out of town on business, he couldn't stop himself from checking up on her and then giving her the third degree when she returned. Needless to say, this was like waving a red flag in her face.

He'd also begun to notice that she was drinking a little more than she normally did, and that her language got pretty raunchy when she drank. He simply could not tolerate that and when he mentioned it to her, she absolutely hit the ceiling. He remembered it as the worst fight they'd ever had.

"Oh, God, Dan. Not only do you want to control every move I make, but now you want to control what goes in and out of my mouth," she said. Their vicious circle had begun. The more he tried to control her, the more she rebelled, and the more rebellious she became, the less secure he felt, and so, of course, the more he tried to control her; on and on, and round and round. My advice to Dan was the same that I give to all Love Addicts. Stop trying to control.

Dan and Jackie: Issue 2—Religion

(And they didn't do their homework!)

Jackie called and came in about two weeks later at Dan's request. She was initially somewhat resistant and reluctant to talk. She was there, she said, because Dan had insisted—but actually, she didn't see much point. The relationship was deteriorating fast. She did eventually warm up and confided that she'd never been in love with anyone like she was this time. She'd been married briefly, but there had never been a physical attraction before like there was with Dan. But she could not *tolerate* walking on eggshells all of the time, especially when they were with other people.

She denied alcohol abuse adamantly, saying that another of their problems was that Dan was raised in a fundamentalist religion and was the world's worst prude. "He has that arrogance that people have who look down on you because you don't believe as they do, do you know what I mean?" she asked.

I assured her that I did, but that I had not been aware of a religious issue in their case. She seemed surprised that Dan had failed to mention this. I asked if she thought a conjoint session could possibly help and she admitted that she'd like to try anything that might help them resolve their differences. She took the structured homework with her and promised to explain it to Dan. Another month passed before they returned together and it was a futile session. Neither had done the homework, and they both seemed at an impasse when they left. I again advised Dan to stop trying to control—what good was it doing anyway? He agreed to try.

I saw them at a restaurant a few weeks later, and we just waved to each other, but Jackie gave me a "thumb's up" sign, and I took that to mean that things had turned around. I would find out later that things had indeed turned around—however, the vicious circle was about to reverse itself.

Dan and Jackie: Issue 3 — Commitment

(And some role reversal, too)

Dan and Jackie came in together about a month later. I was very surprised that they both had done their homework. Surprised, because it had been so long since I had assigned it, I was sure they'd forgotten. Dan seemed calmer, certainly. But Jackie now was the frantic one.

It seems that for a while, things had been going very well. Dan had stopped trying to control, stopped quizzing and questioning, stopped obsessing about Jackie's flirting. How he was able to do that, I don't know. Maybe he had already started to lose interest and it just happened naturally. When *he* stopped, *she* stopped the behavior that was causing the trouble, although probably not on a conscious level.

Now she was enjoying the relationship and wanted to move on to a more permanent arrangement. She wanted children and, at thirty, was well aware of the biological clock. When they exchanged their requests, it became clear that Jackie was now the partner in pursuit. She was pressing for some kind of commitment and Dan was asking for more time.

We identified some of the dysfunctional patterns emerging, and they left with some insight and a little bit of hope.

Actually, *they* had a little bit of hope. I had zero. They had worked so sporadically on the problem that I came close to telling them I didn't think I could help them. How glad I would be later that I didn't.

Dan and Jackie: Failure

Jackie returned alone a few weeks later and seemed just furious at Dan's lack of commitment. They'd been having many conflicts—about religion, about his lack of parenting skills, about finances, and about his ex-wife. She told me that the only reason they were still together was that neither could afford to live alone at this point. I got the distinct impression that she was eager to get on with her life. She gave no indication of depression ... only anger.

Two weeks later, Jackie failed to keep an appointment that she had made. Given the erratic history of the therapy, I was not surprised or alarmed at her absence. I should have been.

Jackie had killed herself two days earlier.

Dan and Jackie: Life Goes On

Dan called me about two weeks later to let me know. I've rarely been so overwhelmed. Suicide of a patient is every therapist's nightmare. Suicide is tragic for anyone who has even been acquainted with the person. One always wonders what they could have said or done, and what signs they missed.

The therapist, as survivor of suicide, is doubly affected. Our patients bare their souls to us, and we, of all people, should have been warned, so we think. It's not always that simple.

For weeks, I pondered and agonized over my failure to pick up the signs of depression that Jackie must have displayed. I could remember none ... there *were* none! Only anger.

I continued to agonize until it finally occurred to me that suicide is a very angry, hostile act. It may, indeed, be the most hostile act a person can commit against a loved one, especially when it is a violent one, as Jackie's was.

I can't describe how and when it happened without compromising the confidentiality of both Jackie and Dan, but I will tell you it was done with a gun. Dan's gun.

Dan came in to see me the other day after he called, and we had a tearful, sad time together. I've spoken with him a few times since that meeting, and I've encouraged him to continue in therapy. God love 'im, he's going to need it.

You are Not to Blame

People close to a suicidal person are not always in a position to analyze all the possible causes of suicide, for suicidal people are not always forthright, and those around them are not all psychics.

No matter how much any of us thinks we know about those around us, they will always remain a mystery. We don't really know what they have been through—how much guilt, shame, and hurt they were already carrying before we entered their lives.

For this reason, it is best to:

1. Try to give as much sincere, positive support as we can handle, while confronting unhealthy behavior in our loved ones.

2. Not blame ourselves for another person's self-destruction, even if it seems to be triggered by an unkind word from our own lips. No one commits suicide over a single word, there is always a backlog of years of pain behind such an act, which is not for us to fix. In most severe addictions, there is a confusion and an intermingling of self-destruction and self-preservation.

Even the most arrogant and independent person among us may be on the verge of self-destruction. We can't presume. What may look to us like a minor irritation, such as losing one's favorite watch or pair of socks, may be the straw that breaks the camel's back for the other person.

Recovering

Breaking Vicious Circles

I don't want to make it sound like stopping vicious circles is always easy, but I also don't want you to think that stopping them is an impossibly difficult task either. The truth is usually somewhere in the middle.

While you may realize that you are not contented with your life as it is and want to pursue wholeness and understanding, your partner may not feel quite the same way. Many people, especially those who have been abused in the past, have a lot at stake in keeping the circle going, or so they may feel. Here's the good news: one person making changes can make a difference for both.

It takes two to tango, and so when you break the circle for *you*, you stop the circle for the other person as well. Of course, this act takes control away from them and will probably make them feel insecure. The moment you destabilize the relationship by saying "No, I quit. I won't play these games any more. I'm sick and tired of it!" the other person only knows that what was their love life is going to disappear, and they don't know what is going to replace it! Looking at it through their perspective, you can see how threatening it is. It could be a stressful time for them, so be prepared for an explosive reaction.

When Greta stopped playing her role with Jason, he got angry and broke up the relationship, but did this mean the therapy didn't work? No, it meant that Jason probably wasn't as ready to heal as Greta was. It was the relationship that didn't work. One might say it failed the test of transformation, and for Greta's life to work, she had to leave the relationship.

We all must secretly fear this great "nothing" out there—a life without human love or support, and it is a great spiritual breakthrough to be able to face that dark night with courage, but when we face it, it is because we are ready. You can't force another person to face it, and so when stopping the circle, try to remember to keep reassuring the other person that you care about them and will always wish them well no matter what, but that you will not support certain behavior that is affecting your life in a terrible way. By separating goodwill, on the one hand, from self-sacrifice and entanglement, on the other, you can make your way through the passageway that leads to freedom, without coming to blows.

Of course, if your partner is as interested in breaking the vicious circle as you are, the chances for change are so much the better.

We seem to be living in a "Twelve-Step" world, with most people recovering —but never recovered—from some sort of obsessive-compulsive behavior or another. Codependency, eating disorders, alcohol, and other drug abuse, gambling, shopping, and dozens of other dysfunctions are all being approached, and self-help is still on the rise. So I'd like to approach the subject of relationships in terms of recovering, rather than recovered. The process of living together with another person requires ongoing work and effort, a process that never ends.

In this section of the book I will present some practical methods for breaking the Vicious Circles in your relationships. First I will offer a series of "exercises" for helping you gain insight into your Vicious Circles, for communicating with your partner about them, and for breaking them. Second is a series of "Topics for Reflection." These are general ideas and hints that it can be very useful to spend some time considering.

EXERCISE 1

Regrets, Requests, and Appreciations

The first exercise involves two worksheets designed to help you recognize the areas in your relationship that need improvement. This exercise should be performed by both you and your partner. You will want to copy the two worksheets so that you can each fill them out separately.

First Statements

Instructions: In the areas below, please list at least 5 statements that reflect your feelings for your partner. Be specific, and feel free to continue on another sheet if needed.

Once you have completed these statements, set aside some time to sit down together to discuss them. This is a tool to help discover where the communication has broken down in the relationship. Remember to use "I" statements when discussing your feelings about these issues (see page 100). If it is difficult for one or both of you to listen to the other, look at Exercise 6 "Styles of Supportive Listening" on page 88 in this section together.

(1) REGRETS: This area should include those things that *you* have done that were harmful to yourself, your partner, or both of you.

I regret _____

I regret _____

I regret _____

I regret _____

I regret _____

(2) REQUESTS: This area should include the things you want your partner to do in order to improve your relationship. Be specific — global statements won't work.

I request _____

I request _____

I request _____

I request _____

I request _____

(3) APPRECIATE: This area should include the things your partner does for you that you appreciate.

I appreciate _____

I appreciate _____

I appreciate _____

I appreciate _____

I appreciate _____

Second Statements

Instructions: Complete the following statements after you have had a chance to discuss your First Statements with each other. Use both your statements and your partner's statements from the previous worksheet.

(1) GOALS: Rewrite your "regrets" stating them now as personal goals. Look carefully at those things you have done that were harmful to yourself, your partner, or both of you, and write "I" statements that are goals for changing that behavior.

I _____

I _____

I _____

I _____

I _____

(2) GIFTS: With your partner, go over their list of requests, and consider how each of you will "gift" the other. With each of your partner's requests, write an "I" statement about how that "gift" will come about.

I _____

I _____

I _____

I _____

I _____

(3) APPRECIATE: Starting with a time period of one week, make a conscious effort to verbalize these appreciations, and all others that come up. This usually gets silly, and people tend to overdo this — that's O.K. — compliment away! When that week is over, set aside a time to discuss how this made both of you feel. Then, try it for another week!

Again, set aside time to discuss what you have written, remembering to listen "reflectively" and use "I" statements.

EXERCISE 2

Bonding

What's Missing in My Relationship?

The following is a good exercise to do every few months, or when problems begin to occur, to help identify where you may need to work and communicate.

There are four modes of relating that couples need to develop constantly in order to find satisfaction in a relationship. Although they each can be somewhat independent of the other, a good marriage needs to include all of them.

Instructions: Read through the *Four Modes of Relating* on the next page. Then, ask yourself the following questions:

1. Which of these four modes of relating are present in your relationship?
2. Which are missing?
3. To what degree of satisfaction are the present modes active?
4. How does the absence of the missing modes make you feel?

Let your partner try this exercise. Compare your responses.

The Four Modes of Relating

1. Friends — The area of friendship is crucial to couples. They need to be able to share, to visit, to make small talk, to play together, to just "hang out."

2. Partners — Couples need to feel a sense of partnership with a fair division of labor and the ability to collaborate and trade off the messy, dirty jobs and tasks.

3. Sweethearts — The courting needs to continue. The hand holding, the verbal and physical affection—affection that *does not* lead to sex. The little notes and cards and phone calls. The dates—dates are very important. People forget this.

4. Lovers — There needs to be a mutual expression of passion with each person feeling the freedom to initiate and express their likes and dislikes. Physical affection that *does* lead to sex but does not obligate one or both.

When the **Friendship** is missing, we feel lonely.

When the sense of **Partnership** is missing, we feel resentment.

When the feeling of being **Sweethearts** is missing, we feel deprived.

When the feeling of being **Lovers** is missing, we feel frustrated.

EXERCISE 3

Styles of Intimacy

Discovering Your *Relationship Vision*

Which of the following best characterizes your relationship?

Just Roomates: Too little intimacy (Functional)
Bowl of Spaghetti: Too much intimacy (Enmeshed)
Master and Servant: Patriarch with wife in orbit, Matriarch with
husband in orbit (Hierarchical)
Happiness: A healthy balance of intimacy and autonomy
(Relational)

Instructions: Now, using the worksheet on the next page, describe your relationship as it will be, when all is as you want it. This is called "The Relationship Vision."

Relationship Vision

Instructions: Make two copies of this form. Let each partner describe the relationship, using the present tense, as it will be when all is as you want it.

Make short, single statements beginning with "We".

Be specific—Set aside a special time to exchange and discuss your lists. Synthesize your two lists into one that each can agree upon. Now, this is an imporant document — type it, sign it, frame it, hang it on the wall, or whatever else gives it validity. Then begin the task of making it real.

1. _____
2. _____
3. _____
4. _____
5. _____
6. _____
7. _____
8. _____
9. _____
10. _____
11. _____
12. _____

EXERCISE 4

Discovering Your Barriers to Intimacy

In working with and balancing your level of intimacy, the following issues are some of the most difficult that couples encounter. Which issues apply to your situation? For each issue that does, set aside a period of a half an hour or more to reflect upon it. Use the *Keep in mind* statements and the suggested readings from the case studies as tools to help your reflection.

1. *Infidelity*. Infidelity may be the greatest and most difficult barrier to get past, due to the level of sadness and hurt it creates. It also evokes many other emotions including shame, fear, insecurity, and anger. *Keep in mind* that infidelity is very common today. (Look at "Love — An Abused Substance")

2. *The inability to forgive and forget*. Infidelity is certainly on the list of things that people are unable to forgive and forget, but by no means is it the only issue. Inability to forgive and forget physical violence, verbal violence, and emotional violence is also a great hurdle. *Keep in mind* that all people make mistakes and some are humdingers, and so the person who can never forgive will always end up totally alone. (Look at "Ring Around the Bedroom — Hide and Seek" and "Moms and Other Back Seat Drivers")

3. *Lack of conflict resolution skills*. One or both partners tend to run away, withdraw, or become hostile. *Keep in mind* that there is no intimacy without risk. (Look at "Love — An Abused Substance")

4. *Fear of transparency*. The fear of appearing weak or foolish. *Keep in mind* that vulnerability is related to lovableness.

5. *Baggage from childhood*. Many times, when we were children, there were severe consequences when we shared honest thoughts and feelings. *Keep in mind* that as our brains store every single memory until we die, great or small, our five-year-old, our ten-year-old self, is still inside us. It matters little that we are not always conscious of it. (Look at any of the "Chronic Circles.")

6. *Basic hostility and mistrust of the opposite sex*. Our history tells us that men/women, as a whole, are dangerous people to confide in. *Keep in mind* that the average male brain works in opposite ways to the average female brain, (or at least uses different software) but they are supposed to co-process, not co-abuse. Remember that you can be the exception to history rather than the rule. (Look at "Moms and Other Back Seat Drivers.")

7. *Emotional immaturity*. Emotionally immature people have no ability for intimacy on a healthy level. *Keep in mind* that people have a tendency to become frozen at the age at which severe untreated trauma occurred. If you act like a five-year-old and you were beaten when you were five, go tell it to a therapist. (Look at "Like Father, Like Son", or read *Abused*)

8. *Unmet personal needs*. Unmet needs promote resentment and hurt, which often results in withdrawal. *Keep in mind* that you are half of the relationship and have a right to speak up. (All of the vicious circles talked about in this book deal with this issue in different ways.)

9. *Poor family of origin models*. When we have no good role models, we simply have no experience in seeing men and women with an attitude of kindness, caring, and sharing. *Keep in mind* that most of what counts in a relationship is nonverbal and can't be learned from a book. (Look at "Like Father, Like Son," "Love, an Abused Substance," or "Ring Around the Bedroom — He Hides and She Seeks.")

There are others. You may want to add to the list.

EXERCISE 5

Levels of Communication

The way we communicate can either sustain or disable a healthy relationship. The levels of communication listed can be operating at the same time, with different issues. Read over the descriptions of the different levels of communication with your partner. Let each partner make a list of how many times you communicate on each level for a predetermined period of time, say, a day, a weekend, or a week. During this time each partner should also keep a diary of communication levels noting the different circumstances under which communication took place, and what level it was on. At the end of the period, compare your findings.

Level 0:
Noncommunication. Withholding information, such as forgetting to say "Your brother called from California." Another form of noncommunication is going out and getting someone else's help because you are avoiding your mate.

Level 1:
Superficial Conversation. Not a real request for information or sharing of ideas. "Hi, how are you," or "How was your day?" and the infamous, "Have a nice day—Thanks, you too" are examples of superficial conversation. There is no emotional risk, as there is no level of intimacy.

Level 2:
Fact-reporting conversation. "Your sister called," "I need new brakes on my car." Still no level of intimacy and no emotional risk.

Level 3:
Ideas and judgments. This is the first level of intimacy, but now there is the risk of conflict, and this may cause a feeling of vulnerability and fear of rejection. "I'd really love to go skiing," "I hate that screechy music." This is the first opportunity for closeness.

Level 4:
Deepest emotions and feelings. "I'm *so* embarrassed about my weight," "I flunked out of college," "My Step-father sexually abused me." With this kind of disclosure, we are really taking a risk. It can be thrown back at us later. But true emotional intimacy is possible when we feel safe enough with our partner to take this risk.

Level 5:
Complete emotional and personal self-disclosure. My wildest fantasies, such as, "I have always had the feeling I would one day live in a castle—be a millionaire—be a famous jazz singer." The marital relationship may not be able to tolerate this level of communication, and you may need to save it for your therapist.

EXERCISE 6

Styles of Supportive Listening

Being able to listen in a positive way is an essential part of communication in any relationship. Read through the following examples of ways of listening, and see if you can recognize your listening "style." Agree with your partner to practice "Reflective Listening" (see below) for a day, or during discussions generated in other sections of this book. This exercise, combined with the "Levels of Communication" exercise, can provide an ongoing way of breaking through vicious circles as they arise.

1. Holding the bucket. A person who "holds the bucket" just simply listens while we unload. Many times this is all we really want or need. No fixing or advising, just supporting. The listener may tell us they are sorry that we're going through this trauma, letting us know that they care, but without putting pressure on us in any way.

2. Reframing. Sometimes, and therapists are famous for this, a statement can be changed into more manageable terms by restating in more positive words. Last week a patient of mine said that she is overly sensitive and gets her feelings hurt very easily. I told her that she is not a superficial person and that she has deep thoughts and feelings. This put the problem in a more positive context and seemed more resolvable to her. It also let her know that being a sensitive person is not necessarily a bad trait.

3. Reflective listening. Reflecting back in paraphrase what you think you heard the other person say, then asking him or her if you got it right. The first speaker says yes or no, and if no, repeats the statement until it is clearly understood. This is the kind of listening skills most often emphasized in relationship therapy.

I often ask each partner to practice reflective listening in the session, and then as a homework assignment, to continue practicing at home.

SOMEWHERE AROUND THE THIRD YEAR OF MARRIAGE ELLEN REALIZED THAT THE MAN WHO WAS **REALLY** HER HUSBAND HAD BEEN LOCKED INSIDE HER FANTASY AND THAT HE HAD TO GO TO THE BATHROOM REAL, REAL BAD.

OFF THE DEEP END © 1992 Andrew Lehman

EXERCISE 7

Strategies for Lending Support

You are not Perfect, and That's O.K.

If strong reaction to change persists, you might point out that you are human and have both the limitations and abilities typical of human beings, and that you would like both respected. It is good to establish that you are not perfect. That takes a lot of pressure off. *But do it verbally rather than by example.* Then establish that you have feelings, and you consider them useful, and don't want them demolished. Then, if the strong reaction persists, be sure to state that you recognize the other person's good points. Establish the other person's self-worth by recalling their best qualities (it has to be convincing) and then bring up the thing that is driving you nuts, in a subtle way. Don't make it sound like an ultimatum, like you're going to leave. The phrase "nobody's perfect" can be very useful.

Reassurance and Honesty

If there's still a reaction, you may have to try to talk to the person and ask if what you said upset them. Reassure the person you meant no harm but were just being honest. If the relationship is employee-employer, there is a chance they'll say, "We appreciate your honesty, here's your severance pay." If you're taking it to this point, you have to be prepared for severance pay. Perhaps this isn't the job for you if you want a healthier life. Employees are often expected to absorb all kinds of abuse at the office with the consequence that they take it out on the kids. Intense physical exercise is the secret stress-dumper of most successful execs. (Like most solutions, moderation is the key in exercising your stress away.)

Positive Attitude

If you are gently trying to confront someone in a personal relationship, try to avoid making the problem you have with that person a "personal problem." The problem is with the problem, it doesn't mean *they* are bad.

With a mate or child, try to hold their hand while you confront the big issues. It's hard to be unfair to someone when you're holding their hand, and they won't feel like they're being "rejected." If you can't hold their hand, compliments are the next best thing. It's also wise to refer to the future in a positive light. Most people secretly fear abandonment of some kind, and a cheery reference to the future may remind them that the world isn't coming apart.

Overcoming Fear

When you are stuck in a personal vicious circle, the first thing to try is to heal the relationship you are in. Most relationships are healed with two things: overcoming fear, and honest communication.

Both parties need to overcome fear of each other, slowly and gradually, before healing can take place. That isn't always so easy. Secondly, and just as important, both parties need to communicate more honestly and more directly if future hurts are to be prevented.

EXERCISE 8

Care and Confrontation

Taking The Risk

In confronting ingrained behavior, you might have to risk some kind of rejection or blame. Best to be prepared for it, be able to say "that's how I feel about it, and I mean it." Often a new response to habitual behavior evokes a hostile reaction at first.

Write a Letter to Yourself

Confrontation is difficult, especially for the people who habitually try to "please" their partners. Writing a letter to yourself first, or perhaps several "position papers" on your own, may help clarify your thinking before you bring the issues up with your partner.

Sometimes we have an urge to take everything back when confronted. Arguments seem to vanish when faced with displeasure. So having it written down first gives us something to refer to if amnesia sets in.

Remember Your Goal

Stopping the activity that keeps the vicious circle going is the only way to break it. This may not be easy at first. If your mate has gotten used to "granting permission" for everything you do and has become high-handed with it, your first act of independence may be greeted with an angry "who said you could do that?" When you answer "that's how I feel about it, it's my right ...", they may hit the roof. It's okay for them to get mad, but you might quietly remove the roof beforehand. If stopping a destructive habit is the goal, it is okay for you to be the cause of their anger. What's more, it's okay for them to be angry! Knowing that whatever happens will be okay, even if everyone gets mad, is one way of removing the roof!

One Step at a Time

Addressing problems relating to the vicious circle one at a time is easier and more effective than trying to change "everything" at once. In the case of the people who can never complain until trapped at the end, the strategy is simple, though not easy. Break the pattern by tactfully addressing small problems, and then work towards addressing bigger ones, as you become more comfortable with the process. Again, if the pattern is a habit that has evolved over a long period of time, don't expect immediate gratitude.

The Last Option – Opting Out

The concept of a good relationship as a contraption stuck together with crazy glue is not a very encouraging concept of "relationship". Vicious circles are habitual and stem from habitual behavior. A new response on your part to habitual behavior by the other person will generally evoke a hostile reaction at first. It is true that if you think about your own most ingrained habits, you might feel threatened and hostile, too, if you no longer knew how to act in your relationship. This is where collaboration and change can begin, with both partners taking the risk to work together.

But if the destructive behavior of your partner continues, and there is no change in the problem areas of your relationship, except the effort you are putting out yourself, you may need to opt out. Remember Bob and Susan and Kevin and Kim and "The Old Eggshell Routine" — sometimes the hurt and the destructive activity have gone too far or gone on for too long, and it is no longer possible or even advisable to continue with the relationship.

You can't stop someone else from the habit of smoking or drinking, although you may often think you can. But you can stop a habit-cycle-built-for-two at any time and effectively stop the other person. This may work within the relationship, and it may not. Sometimes, the only way to heal a relationship is to leave. It is best to prepare yourself as many ways as possible, but do it.

Often the best way to change our relationships is to change our ideas about them. The following topics are vehicles for personal reflection about our ideas and relationships.

You can work with these topics by setting aside a period of time — say a half an hour a day — to devote to reflection, one day per topic. Read the passage detailing the topic over a few times. Think about how the topic applies to your situation. Keep a diary or notebook on hand and jot down what comes to mind.

If your partner is willing, have him or her practice "reflecting" with you. It is a good idea to read the passage together, but to conduct your reflecting sessions separately and in silence. When the time you have set aside is over, share your responses.

TOPIC 1

Hard Work but Worth It

As you have likely noticed in reading the various case histories, I'm a pretty active therapist. Most therapy these days must be brief due to constraints from Insurance Companies and Managed Care. So therapists must be active in order to get the process moving and the focus onto solutions.

I always tell my couples that I'm going to work them to death. They think that's pretty funny, until they discover how near the truth that really is. But therapy of any kind is hard work, and one definition of work is "doing that which you are unaccustomed to doing." It takes committed people to do that. The exercises presented in this section of the book give you the opportunity to do this work with each other.

I personally believe that in order for a couple to make headway, there must be a certain level of intelligence. It also seems to be necessary for maturity to have developed. Without maturity, there is too much rigidity for change to take place. That's what breaking vicious circles is all about — change.

The first thing you must ask is "what are your true feelings for each other?" You need to establish whether you want to enrich your partnership, or if you are "stopping by on the way down to the courthouse." When one of you says, "I can't stand to be in the same room with him" or the other says, "I'm not in love with her any more," I don't have much hope for the relationship. Although we can do a lot of good work in terms of changing behavior, teaching communication skills, identifying and stopping the vicious circles, our feelings are a given and we don't have much control over them. This said, it is true that when behaviors change and communication improves, and when vicious circles are identified and stopped, then feelings can change too. But not always.

This section of the book includes some very structured work. It can be a relief to have something "real" to do. Also, it is important to make *specific* commitments. If there is an extra-marital affair, violence, drugs, alcohol abuse, it must stop. Neither the work in this book nor therapy can overcome these roadblocks.

I've already mentioned a few of the techniques, such as "defusers," for disarming the escalation of conflicts, and the "I statement" exercise, which is invaluable in getting to the specifics of the problematic issues. These techniques are in the following pages. There are also many other rebuilding tools, some are my own invention, and some are borrowed from other therapists. There are many good clinicians coming up with new techniques and tools. One tool not in this book, but a good one, "marriage encounter weekends" or "retreats," have helped countless couples to enrich their relationships.

TOPIC 2

Even Committed Couples Get the Blues

Even a marriage "made in heaven" has to work down here on the ground as well, and there will most likely be disputes and conflicts. It's comic relief to me that the word "marital," pertaining to marriage, and the word "martial," pertaining to war, are so very similar. The only difference is where the "I" is placed. This may sound overly simplistic but keeping boundaries and desires in perspective (where the "I" is placed) is the key to having a healthy relationship. The following examples show how an unhealthy "I" can erode a healthy relationship.

It Takes Two "I's" To See Clearly

When too much emphasis is placed on the "I" by both partners, there tends to be a serious control issue to resolve. Each tends to out-do the other with demands rather than out-doing one another by being loving and thoughtful. This is communication breakdown in the fast lane!

Imbalanced "I's"

On the other hand, when only one partner is demanding, and the other is only "giving," there is an inevitable build up of anger and resentment by the giving partner. No matter how quiet and patient that partner is, you can guarantee that something will "give" sooner or later; they will either leave or explode, or start undermining the relationship as if tunneling to freedom.

When too little emphasis is placed on "I" by both partners, both people fail to get their needs met and then feel resentful towards each other. This, too, is a common breakdown.

Guilt and Blame Contests

Another way that couples lose their balance on the "I" beam is through guilt and blame contests. When too little emphasis is put on the "I" as in "I am not responsible for my life," one tends to project that responsibility onto the other and become blaming. It takes two to tangle, and so one is never sure with whom the real cause lies. Laying guilt traps does little to cement warm, close bonds of friendship between lovers but does often cement ties of anxiety and fear, if that's what you want. M. Scott Peck, in *The People of the Lie*, pointed out that once an individual can no longer see his or her own shadow side, they can quickly become evil. The typical concept most people have of an evil person is one who continually blames others and never themselves.

Just as destructive is the person who puts too much emphasis on their own guilt, though few will point it out. The guilt-ridden person often brings out the worst in people, rather than the best. Guilty-feeling people often become targets and victims and attract more reasons to feel guilty. Such guilt can cripple the ability to enjoy life, which spells frustration for others.

Guilt can be used as a way to control others just as much as blame can be. This kind of humility is really self-centered and leads to vicious circles. It is another way in which couples put "I" in the wrong place.

TOPIC 3

Win-Win Communication

The chief complaint from most of the couples I've seen in my practice is "We don't communicate!" There are many issues they don't communicate about; sex, kids, money, in-laws, division of labor at home, infidelity, on and on, but poor communication skills are invariably what leads to conflicts.

To quote the well-known communications expert, Dr. Bonnie Gene Ritter,

> "We tend to believe that conflict requires a winner and a loser. When we struggle in a relationship to determine who the loser will be, the relationship itself weakens and both participants become losers. We can learn to negotiate or 'fight' within the relationship for a stronger bond with at least two winners!"

In order to learn to accomplish this grand feat, communication patterns have to change. Typically, one partner is passive and the other aggressive, or both are passive or aggressive. All of these combinations are deadly for a relationship.

The trick is for *both* to become **assertive**, and my definition for this is:

1. expressing feelings;
2. asking for what you need *without hostility*;
3. and this may be the crucial part—*at the time it occurs*.

The secret is in expressing this using "I" statements. "You" statements are threatening, but "I" statements generally are not. "You slob, you never pick up your socks" can lead to a struggle. "I feel taken advantage of when I have to pick up other people's socks" probably will not. "You" statements tend to lead to an "attack/defend" mode, and a dreadful vicious circle begins, even in the best of relationships.

TOPIC 4

The Three Stages of Healing

To make sense out of the healing process, I feel it helps to make sense out of the sickness. What are the roots of the sickness? What made it necessary? What are the good points? If you look deep enough, illnesses are usually trying to tell us something. The codependent person is only ill to the extent that they need healing, but that illness is a way of coping with a previous or ongoing hazard, just as the physical immune system is.

The analysis of healing into the following stages can be helpful in understanding the way healing can work for an individual and in a relationship.

Stage One: Acting Out

At the beginning of the healing process, the hidden motives and insecurities, the hidden lacks in self-esteem, become outwardly apparent in arguments, power plays, and addictions. This stage is parallel to the stage in physical healing where an undiagnosed illness begins to show symptoms. During this stage, the relationship, like a diseased body, becomes more and more toxic, more and more poisonous, and vicious circles form; hate begets hate, frustration begets frustration. This "acting out" is not all bad, but if and only if it leads the couple into some form of treatment. The "real" problem is each individual's own underlying weakness, not just the little fights and squabbles. That is why we can say that the acting out is not "bad." Most diseases are not discovered until symptoms occur, and psychological diseases often show up in relationships rather than coughs and sneezes. The kind of toxic behavior we have been looking at up until now can help us diagnose the underlying chronic vicious circles so we can ask ourselves the right questions.

Stage Two: Healing Crisis

The second stage is the healing crisis stage. Generally, there is going to be some strong medicine needed. The diet must change, perhaps doing without favorite foods. Perhaps the person needs to jog or do some sort of rigorous exercise to get better. It is sometimes an unpleasant stage, but we go through it because we trust the wisdom of the doctor (or "medicine person") or the healing process itself and we want to enjoy the benefits of good health somewhere down the road. Unfortunately, it often gets worse before it gets better, and this is what a healing crisis is all about. Sometimes the symptoms go crazy just before the fever breaks.

In terms of relationships, this stage is crucial to recovery. The therapist often will recommend some sort of emotional "fasting," such as not seeing each other at all, or seeing each other under carefully limited circumstances. In a way it is like going back to the beginning of the circle and starting all over again. Like the needle on a record, you can't run the record backwards exactly, but you can pick up the needle and start over again, and do it right the next time.

After a period of "emotional fasting," which may involve a short period of celibacy, a complete control of verbal abuse, careless language, and forms of physical abuse, the couple finally reaches the baseline of their relationship, the baseline of friendship and comradeship, relatively free of addictive behavior. The couple should feel that an emotional cleansing has taken place. Then they gradually begin to resume their "normal" lives, but this time consciously defusing the obsessive-compulsive behavior that spoiled the mix the last time.

Stage Three: Wholeness

The third stage of healing is finding a new and sustainable life style that can be lived with, a lifestyle that involves a balance between vigilance and comfort. In the new lifestyle, one enjoys small indulgences once in a while but, on the whole, avoids addictions of all kinds and plans regular "checkups." In terms of relationships, the doctor is the therapist, a self-help book, a support group meeting, or a talk with a spiritual counselor or good friend.

The third stage for an abusive couple also involves a balance between vigilance and comfort. The old "norm" is not good enough. The couple must find a new "norm" if they expect to find happiness where happiness has been lost.

Just as some people get stuck in the "acting out" stage, other couples get stuck in the healing stage and are never able to enjoy each other's company again. Still others take a while to find a comfortable third stage for themselves and become like new converts, always lecturing others, while struggling to maintain their own discipline. When all is said and done, it is best to be yourself, and to return to some version of stage two when things get out of balance.

The key to maintaining good relationships is that *everything* is a relationship, between the man and woman, between the couple and their children, between the family with their relatives, the relatives and the community and society in general. Working on one means working on the others too, as one effects the others — so healing within one relationship can have many positive results in the other relationships in anyone's life.

TOPIC 5

The Vicious Circle is Not the Relationship

It is important to remember when trying to break a vicious circle that the vicious circle itself is not the relationship. I know of one relationship between two women who worked together. One of the women was always trying to please the other, who would "permit" her to do things. When the pleaser finally made a meek plea for independence, the permitter, who was a rather unstable woman, connived to get her friend fired. But the pleaser never went back on her decision and felt better about herself because of it.

You may ask how such a relationship could be saved—truth is, there never was a relationship. If there were, the "permitter" would eventually give in a little and listen to reason.

In another case, a woman's uncle and relatives each felt entitled to have her "clear" all her proposed activities and travels with them first. When she went out on her own, instead of saying, "Sorry. It won't happen again," she said, "I am an adult, I have my rights! I'm the only one who can live my life. We are equals. That's the way I feel about it."

Her answer upset a very old, ingrained family behavior habit, and more than one person hit the roof. They threatened and made her an outcast and threw in old dirty laundry, mixed in with a few skeletons, to be sure. Still, the woman stuck to her guns and felt cleaner and healthier than she had before. Eventually, the relatives softened up. They had no choice.

TOPIC 6

The Differences Can Work to Complement Each Other

Through recognizing your own patterns, accommodating, defusing, loving, communicating, listening, bonding, supporting, confronting, by healing your own past and becoming more complete as an individual, you can make the differences between you and your mate work to your advantage.

Learn to make the differences compliment each other. When you figure out how to do that, you will have discovered the key to a healthy relationship.

Anna Beth and Ted

Anna Beth is a C.P.A. and a whiz at financial affairs, while her husband, Ted, is a creative guy who builds sturdy furniture and cabinets, keeps a beautifully landscaped yard, and can repair nearly anything, including the cars. Each of them recognizes the other's talents and contributions to the partnership and praises the other generously. Their marriage is working.

Sue and Eddie

Sue and Eddie have similar talents, only she tends to ridicule him because he doesn't have enough sense to balance the checkbook and has no interest in their business affairs. He feels defensive and berates her for being a slob.

If the two parties can accept the fact that they are simply human beings with both good *and* unhealthy characteristics and can accept the differences as positive while recognizing the other person's talents, then they will be able to grow together. If one or both insist that the other is flawed because of their differences, there is little chance of saving the relationship.

I'd like to make it clear that the dynamics described throughout this book refer to what might be called "normal" couples. If there is alcohol or other drug use, gambling, infidelity, chronic lying, violence—either verbal or physical or both, then the dysfunctional patterns are multiplied. If children are present, then their on-the-job training to become a dysfunctional mate is well underway. Not only are we looking at vicious circles in one family, but at the possible dysfunctional patterns for generations to come.

TOPIC 7

Completing the Circle

In my years as a "relationship therapist," I have not met a couple that one could call "perfect"—completely healthy in the emotional sense. In one way or another, there are always individual differences that cause conflicts to some degree. If these differences are acute, then violence, either physical or verbal, or both, can result.

If the differences are subtle and only mildly chronic, then there may be periods of silence, physical and emotional withdrawal, as well as some cutting and snide remarks bantered back and forth. All of these behavior patterns erode the quality of life for each of the partners, and can, over time, ruin any relationship.

Each of the case histories presented earlier in this book represent one or more of the dysfunctional behavior patterns that undermine relationships through vicious circles. However, we know that the relationship didn't start out that way, or they probably never would have gotten together in the first place. The longer I work in this field, the more amazed I am at how people do get together in the first place. When they come for therapy, it sounds as if they never had anything in common. The fact is, what they have in common — what brought them together in the first place — is hidden beneath the vicious circle that is tearing them apart.

TOPIC 8

"Love is Exquisite Kindness"

Most couples start their relationships with a physical attraction to the other. "Mother Nature's Plan" gets us moving towards fulfilling this attraction, and if all goes well, the courting ritual begins. I've heard this called the Restaurant Phase of relationship development. At the Restaurant Phase, each person is on his and her best behavior and appears totally infatuated with the other. They may want to be with the object of their affection as much as possible and are miserable when they are not.

This mutual attraction lasts only so long, and often one of the partners loses this state of emotional bliss before the other does. It is at this point in the relationship that the real people show up.

If mutual attraction for the other has faded quickly, they will simply drift apart. Although friendships sometime develop, they may not choose to see each other again. Friends hear such remarks as "He/she just wasn't my type," "We didn't have as much in common as we thought," "I don't know what I saw in him/her in the first place," etc.

But if mutual infatuation lasts for any length of time, marriage or living together generally follows. The important thing to remember is that the "restaurant phase" of a relationship has no more to do with real love than any other phase. The best part of love comes after the wining and dining. Joseph Campbell, in one of his interviews with Bill Moyers on PBS stated, "Love is exquisite kindness." That statement makes sense to me, for when we are kind, courteous, gracious, and respectful of each other, then what is called love can flourish, and both members of the relationship can be enriched.

This simple key to relationship development is difficult to grasp because most of us have not experienced such behavior as children. We just did not have adequate role models, our parents, from which to learn. They had no adequate role models either, from which to learn, and on and on, 'round and 'round. This is how *intergenerational* vicious circles are perpetuated.

For some, the models were very toxic and dangerous, complete with verbal and physical abuse. In other less toxic models, one or both of the parents may have been overly controlling, overly critical, overly blaming and shaming, and essentially poor models to learn from, especially in the area of developing healthy relationships. One important factor to consider is that not all children in a family, regardless of the level of dysfunction, internalize the problems of the family in the same way. Nor do they manifest the set of problems in their own adult lives in the same manner or to the same degree.

Like many others, I strongly believe that our basic personality structure is something that we bring along with us to this life. It's called genetics, and genes and hormones are determiners of how we will react to our environment. But the fact is that we will react to our environment in one way or another. It explains why two children raised in the same dysfunctional family turn out so differently.

One man I have seen in my office is a federal judge, and I don't know many people who are higher achievers than he is. His brother, who is ten months older, is a junkie, and currently a guest of the state of Texas in the penitentiary. Both men have suffered the dreadful long-term affects of an abusive childhood. My high achieving client is a closet alcoholic and, although very fair on the bench, is a terror at home with his wife and children.

However it is that children become flawed, they march into their adulthood with varied degrees of ability—or disability—in the area of healthy relationships. None of us is exempt from this dynamic.

We often bring fantasies, unreasonable expectations, faulty preconceptions, and delusional thinking into the formation of our relationships. When our partner does not conform, we are confused, angry, perplexed, and resentful that the love of our life is such a disappointment.

This is when people "fall out of love." The most common statement I hear in my office is "I still love you, but I'm just not in love with you any more."

Personally, I think the term "in love" (especially when two people are hardly acquainted) translates into "a temporary state of insanity." Call it euphoria, if you like, but it can't last—we couldn't stand it. We couldn't get on with our lives, our professions, our parenting, and all the rest.

It must mature into that "exquisite kindness" state. And when a person leaves such a relationship for an "in love" euphoria, which will also end, he or she is likely to be hopping around forever, searching for yet another "in love."

I repeat, the longer I do this work, the more amazed I am at how people ever get together in the first place. It seems that opposites do attract, as we've heard all our lives. Maybe we marry to complete ourselves, I don't know, but it seems that the things that attract people to each other in the beginning are the very things that they butt heads over, and which comes between them in the end. It is making the commitment to discover the connections beneath the difficulties that allow us to decide if this relationship is really "right" for us and move forward in mutual support and "exquisite kindness".

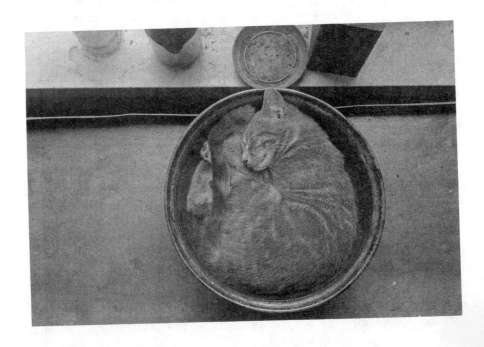

One Last Word—Celebrate the Progress

We tend to live for instant gratification.

When couples are in therapy, they tend to become impatient for instant healing. It doesn't always happen. There will be progress, but there will also be setbacks. It's human nature to revert back to old ways and comfortable patterns. But they usually recognize when this occurs, and therein lies the element for change. Just this week, for example, a couple I have been seeing for a short time was lamenting over the "back and forth" progress they've been making, and I was trying to encourage them by telling them how common this setback syndrome can be. She got an enlightened look on her face and said, "You're right. We continue to focus on the things that still need work and forget to celebrate the progress!"

By all means, look for the strengths you each have, as well as the strengths you have as a couple. That is where the building will begin.

Celebrate the Progress!

APPENDIX

*Marital Separation Contract**

I _____ agree to a marital separation from my spouse for _____ weeks during which time I will not make any final decisions to either divorce or remain married. I agree to the following stipulations:

Therapy—I will attend weekly conjoint marital therapy sessions for the duration of this contract. I will initiate individual therapy as I prefer and in consideration of my therapist's recommendations.

Contact With Spouse—I will spend time with my partner on _____ occasions per week. I will have telephone contact with my spouse only to arrange our "dates" and in the case of an emergency. I will make no effort to see my spouse more frequently than the designated rate.

Sexual Contact With Spouse—I understand that my partner and I _____ continue having sexual contact with one another and that (n)either of us has the right to initiate sexual activity.

Dating—I understand that each of us _____ eligible to date others (and there are no restrictions on whom to date or where a date may be conducted).

Sexual Contact With Others—I understand that both my partner and I _____ eligible to have sexual relations with others during the contracted separation period.

Privacy—I will make no effort to oversee the activities of my spouse, "drop in" or telephone except as specified above.

Contact With Children—(_____) I agree to spend individual time with my children at least weekly. I will arrange to take my children overnight unless travel with my work prevents me from doing so.

Financial Support—

Homework—I will make every effort to carry out the homework assignments to which I have agreed during therapy sessions. I understand that my marital relationship, as well as my personal growth, is to have priority during this separation period. I will use only positive methods to encourage my spouse to participate in doing homework.

Renegotiation—I will participate in renegotiating the separation contract at the end of this contract period should my spouse and I, in collaboration with our therapist, prefer to sustain the separation period. Furthermore, should either my partner or I wish to alter any part of this contact at any time, it is to be discussed and re-negotiated during a therapy session with our therapist.

SIGNED_____

SIGNED_____

WITNESS_____

DATE_____

* It is recommended that this contract be used in a marital therapy setting.

About the Author

Dee Anna Parrish is a psychiatric social worker with extensive experience in individual, couple, and family counseling. She specializes in working with adults who were raised in dysfunctional families — adult children of alcoholics, children of physical, sexual, verbal, and emotional abusers, and children of parents who abused through neglect and deprivation. Ms. Parrish is currently in private practice in Dallas and is affiliated with Human Affairs International.

Good Grief Rituals
Tools for Healing

ELAINE CHILDS-GOWELL

As a psychotherapist with over twenty year's experience, the author realized that the emotion of grief was not limited to bereavement but was in fact experienced in an extraordinary range of circumstances, from natural disasters to the end of a love affair. In this sane, comforting, and deeply thoughtful book, she offers the reader a series of simple grief rituals, among them the venting of feelings, letter writing, affirmations, exercises to act out negative emotions as well as forgiveness, fantasies, meditations, and more. Adult chidren of alcoholics and dysfunctional families, victims of incest and assult, and those who've lost a pet, wrecked a car, or suffered any kind of loss will find that these "good grief rituals" move them through loss to forgiveness and, ultimately, to gratitude and a new sense of life.

ELAINE CHILDS-GOWELL, RN, MN, MPH, Ph.D., considers herself a "spiritual midwife". She has been teaching, and doing psychotherapy for more than 20 years. She currently works as a Clinical Transactional Analyst in Seattle, with individuals, couples, families, and groups. Elaine is known in the Northwest, Canada, Europe and in TA circles generally as a workshop leader, and particularily for her work relating to Transactional Analysis with the body.

$8.95p, ISBN 0-88268-118-4; 112 pages, 6 x 6 ½.

How to Forgive When You Don't Know How

Jacqui Bishop and Mary Grunte

In this groundbreaking look at the psychology of forgiveness, the authors show how resentment—toward other people, toward one's self, even toward God—can consume precious emotional energy and seriously impair both self-esteem and the ability to experience joy. Drawing on the healing techniques used so successfully in *HOW TO LOVE YOURSELF WHEN YOU DON'T KNOW HOW*, they offer a short program for accelerating the process of forgiveness, including visualization, emotional discharge, searching back, and prayer. Enlivened with classic quotations on the nature of forgiveness, this revolutionary book explodes long-standing myths—including the notion that forgiveness involves self-denial, making up, confessing, or turning the other cheek.

JACQUI BISHOP and MARY GRUNTE are the authors of *HOW TO LOVE YOURSELF WHEN YOU DON'T KNOW HOW: Healing All Your Inner Children*. A psychologist and psychiatric nurse respectively, they both live in White Plains, New York.

$7.95p, ISBN 0-88268-142-7; 126 pages, 6 X 6½, b&w photos.